HOW GOD HEALS WITHOUT DOCTORS, MEDICINE, OR SURGERY

ALSO FROM REVIVAL TODAY

Financial Overflow

Dominion Over Sickness and Disease

Boldly I Come: Praying According to God's Word

Twenty Secrets for an Unbreakable Marriage

How to Dominate in a Wicked Nation

Seven Wrong Relationships

Everything a Man Should Be

Understanding the World in Light of Bible Prophecy

Are You Going Through a Crisis?

The 20 Laws that Govern the Financial Anointing

35 Questions for Those Who Hate the Prosperity Gospel

The Art of Spiritual Warfare

How God Heals without Doctors, Medicine, or Surgery

Books are available in EBOOK and PAPERBACK through your favorite online book retailer or by request from your local bookstore.

HOW GOD HEALS WITHOUT DOCTORS, MEDICINE, OR SURGERY

JONATHAN SHUTTLESWORTH
ADALIS SHUTTLESWORTH

Without limiting the rights under copyright(s) reserved below, no part of this publication may be reproduced, stored in, or introduced into a retrieval system, or transmitted in any form or by any means (electronic, mechanical, photocopying, recording, or otherwise) without the prior permission of the publisher and the copyright owner.

For Educational, Informational, and Spiritual Purposes Only. The information provided in or through this book is for educational, informational, and spiritual purposes only and is made available to you for your own use.

Not a Substitute for Medical Advice. The information provided in or through this book is not intended to be a substitute for professional medical advice, diagnosis or treatment (including doctor/physician, nurse, physician's assistant, or any other health professional), Mental Health Provider (including psychiatrist, psychologist, therapist, counselor, or social worker), registered dietitian or licensed nutritionist, or member of the clergy.

Consult Your Physician or Health Care Provider. Our intent is NOT to replace any relationship that exists or should exist, between you and your Medical Provider or Mental Health Provider. You should always seek the advice of your doctor/physician, nurse practitioner, physician's assistant, Mental Health Provider, or another health care professional regarding any questions or concerns about your specific health situation. You shall not disregard professional medical advice or delay seeking professional advice because of information you have read or received from us. You should not stop taking any medications without speaking to your Medical Provider and/or Mental Health Provider. If you have or suspect that you have a medical problem, you are advised to contact your Medical Provider or Mental Health Provider promptly.

No Warranties. WE MAKE NO REPRESENTATIONS OR WARRANTIES OF ANY KIND, EXPRESS OR IMPLIED, AS TO THE INFORMATION, CONTENT, MATERIALS, PROGRAMS, PRODUCTS OR SERVICES INCLUDED IN THIS BOOK. TO THE FULL EXTENT PERMISSIBLE BY APPLICABLE LAW, WE DISCLAIM ALL WARRANTIES, EXPRESS OR IMPLIED, INCLUDING IMPLIED WARRANTIES OF MERCHANTABILITY AND FITNESS FOR A PARTICULAR PURPOSE. WE WILL NOT BE LIABLE FOR ANY DAMAGES OF ANY KIND ARISING FROM INFORMATION CONTAINED IN THIS BOOK.

Not Evaluated by the FDA. The information contained in this book has not been evaluated by the Food and Drug Administration.

Accuracy. Although every effort is made to ensure the accuracy of information shared in this book, the information may inadvertently contain inaccuracies or typographical errors. We are not responsible for the views, opinions, or accuracy of facts referenced in or through this book. Every effort has been made to present you with the most accurate, up-to-date information. The scanning, uploading, and distributing of this book via the internet or any other means without the permission of the publisher and copyright owner is illegal and punishable by law. Please purchase only authorized copies, and do not participate in or encourage piracy of copyrighted materials. Your support of the author's rights is appreciated.

The scanning, uploading, and distributing of this book via the internet or any other means without the permission of the publisher and copyright owner is illegal and punishable by law. Please purchase only authorized copies, and do not participate in or encourage piracy of copyrighted materials. Your support of the author's rights is appreciated.

Unless otherwise indicated, Scriptures are taken from the HOLY BIBLE, NEW LIVING TRANSLATION(NLT): Scriptures taken from the HOLY BIBLE, NEW LIVING TRANSLATION, Copyright ©1996, 2004, 2007 by Tyndale House Foundation. Used by permission of Tyndale House Publishers, Inc., Carol Stream, Illinois 60188. All rights reserved. Used by permission.

Scriptures marked NKJV are taken from the NEW KING JAMES VERSION (NKJV): Scripture taken from the NEW KING JAMES VERSION®. Copyright© 1982 by Thomas Nelson, Inc. Used by permission. All rights reserved. Scriptures marked KJV are taken from the KING JAMES VERSION (KJV): KING JAMES VERSION, public domain.

Scriptures marked (AMPC) are taken from the Amplified® Bible (AMPC), Copyright © 1954, 1958, 1962, 1964, 1965, 1987 by The Lockman Foundation. Used by permission. lockman.org

Copyright © 2024 by Revival Today. All rights reserved.

Released: June 2024

978-1-64457-754-7   Paperback
978-1-64457-755-4   Hardcover

Rise UP Publications
644 Shrewsbury Commons Ave
Ste 249
Shrewsbury PA 17361
United States of America
www.riseUPpublications.com
Phone: 866-846-5123

CONTENTS

Introduction	11
CHAPTER 1	13
A Solid Foundation in The Word of God	
God Wants You Healed	16
God's Plan for You	18
God's Formula	21
Confession	22
Questions	23
CHAPTER 2	25
Sickness Is Spiritual	
Sickness Comes from the Devil	26
Let's Talk About Job	29
Develop a Hatred for Sickness and Disease	30
Confession	31
Questions	33
CHAPTER 3	35
Every Spiritual Blessing—Including Healing—Belongs to You	
Healing Is Spiritual	36
Faith for Healing	40
Your Covenant with God Includes Divine Health	48
Strength in Old Age	52
A Long Life	54
You Have an Inheritance	54
Confession	56
Questions	57
CHAPTER 4	59
Take Your Healing by Force	
A Lack of Knowledge Destroys Lives	59
Confession	64
Questions	65

CHAPTER 5 — 67
Seven Hindrances to Divine Healing
1. Pride — 67
2. Wickedness — 68
3. Bitterness — 69
4. Anger — 71
5. No Rest — 72
6. No Joy — 73
7. No Regard for Your Own Health — 74
Confession — 75

Questions — 77

CHAPTER 6 — 79
How to Cooperate with God for Healing and a Long Life
1. Do You Have a Food Addiction? — 80
2. Understand the Connection Between the FDA and the Pharmaceutical Industry — 81
3. Fewer Calories Is Not Necessarily the Answer — 82
4. A Healthy Lifestyle Brings Energy, Flexibility, and Strength — 83
5. Be Fair to Your Spouse — 83
6. Avoid Soda — 83
7. Reduce or Eliminate Fast Food — 84
8. Reduce Sugar — 85
9. Eliminate Alcohol — 85
10. Move — 85
11. Don't Be a Diet Freak — 86
12. Consider Intermittent Fasting — 86
13. Fight Social Norms — 87
14. Start Where You Are, God Will Help You — 87
Confession — 88

Questions — 89

CHAPTER 7 — 91
Communion Carries Power
A Happy Meal — 95
Confession — 97

Questions — 99

CHAPTER 8   101
Healing Testimonies
Cancer and Kidneys Healed!   101
Paralyzed Woman Healed from Rare Genetic Diseases   103
39 Tumors Completely Disappeared   105
Bonus Testimony From Marissa – Another Cancer Patient Healed   107
Heart Condition Healed and Lungs Restored!   108
Healed From Lupus   109
Chronic Pain Vanished   110
Heart Condition Healed   111
Blind Eye Restored   112
Woman Healed of Leukemia   113
Young Man Restored After Severe Accident   114
Toddler Healed from Respiratory Attack   115

Answer Key   117
Notes   121
Author Photo   123
About the Author   124

INTRODUCTION

Prepare yourself for one of the most impactful books on healing that you've ever read. This book will help you out of whatever condition you're in, whether it's a physical sickness or a mental illness. It doesn't matter what you're going through; the blessing of God and the Word of God will pull you out. The Bible says that His Word was sent and it healed them, and this book is your point of contact with that truth. The Word of God will bring healing and wholeness to your body.

I speak from personal experience, having endured a time when my body seemed unresponsive to my deepest desires for healing. I faced a daunting challenge where even the prospect of a new day felt unbearable. The medical experts had no solutions for my affliction. However, it was the Word of God that rescued me. I was not only physically unwell but mentally tormented with fear and panic, oppressed by the Devil. Yet, it was God's Word that emerged as my true remedy.

Whatever situation you're facing, however bleak it might seem, whatever the doctors have said—they may have sent you home like they sent me home without a diagnosis or remedy—know that the Word of God has the power to overcome every obstacle and every sickness and disease in your life. It doesn't matter if you've been diagnosed with bipolar disorder, depression, cancer, or the inability to be fruitful. It doesn't matter what the problem is. God has already healed you, and this book will guide you step by step toward gaining access to the reality of your healing that was given through the blood of Jesus 2000 years ago on the cross.

Do you know that healing is already yours? You don't have to pray for it. If you're a born-again child of God, all you need to do is say, "God, you did this for me. It's already been done. I receive it now." The Bible says in Hosea 4:6 that my people perish because of a lack of understanding. This book will chip away at your lack of understanding. Lack of understanding keeps you from receiving the fullness of what God has in store for you.

After you read this book, I believe you will receive your healing. It doesn't matter if you've been dealing with your affliction for two hours or 25 years. God will show up because of the newfound knowledge you have discovered in His Word, in Jesus' name.

Adalis Shuttlesworth, Pastor

CHAPTER 1

A SOLID FOUNDATION IN THE WORD OF GOD

You need a solid foundation of the Word of God to receive your healing. Every believer must have a firm foundation of what the Word says about healing, whether you're currently experiencing sickness or not.

Don't be too quick to forget what life was like in 2020. There was a dark, heavy spirit prevalent throughout the globe. I still remember what it felt like to step out of my home and feel evil all around me. The only way to escape that evil unscathed is to have the light of God's Word illuminate through the darkness.

Covid-19 illustrated the fact that most people either don't know the Word of God or they know it and don't truly believe it. Although many people knew and could recite Psalm 91, those same people allowed their minds to take over during Covid-19. They allowed a spirit of fear and darkness to overtake them.

Covid-19 is not the last attack this world will face. What will you do if the Spanish Flu or the Black Plague returns? Will you lock yourself in a basement with an AK-47 and powdered milk?

The only reason people are sick, or experience failure and stagnation is because they have not received the Word of God to illuminate the darkness in their lives. Your firm foundation on the Word of God will be the source of light in a very dark world, not only for you but also for your children, your loved ones, and even your coworkers. That foundation gives you the confidence to disregard what's happening around you because you have a light. You know exactly where you're going. You have a mandate and a call on your life, and ultimately, nothing can stop you.

It's crucial that you receive these fundamental truths of the Word of God because it will sustain you through any trial you face in life. I can confirm this from personal experience. The Word of God has literally brought me back to life. It has brought me through the darkest times of my life, and I want it to do the same for you.

I wish I had the time to speak with you personally. But since I can't, this is my way of communicating with you. I may not know your exact situation, but if there's darkness in your life of any kind, God wants to shed His light on it. I allowed His light to wash over me, and God began to reveal things to me.

James 1:17 says,

> Every good gift and every perfect gift is from above, and comes down from the Father of lights, with whom there is no variation or shadow of turning.
>
> —James 1:17 (NKJV)

God's light is what you need to expel the darkness you're in right now. At my darkest moments, I chose to get into the Word, and it began to take effect in my body. Suddenly, I was strong in my mind and in my body. I thought, 'Wow, it really is that easy,' and God's response to me was, "Yes, now go tell everyone."

Soon after, I had a glimpse of myself in a dark room. I kept hitting the wall, and I could feel my face was full of blood. I thought to myself, 'I'm hurting. What's going on?' Then I heard the Holy Spirit's voice say, "Turn on the light." As soon as He said it, I turned on the light, saw the door, and I left the room. Yes, I was bloody and beaten, but all I had to do to leave the darkness was turn on the light and walk out.

That's all it takes to be healed. Turn on the light of God's Word. His Word is a lamp unto your feet and a light unto your path (Psalm. 119:105). He is light. If you're surrounded by darkness, all you must do is turn on the light by finding what the Word says about your circumstance.

Stand on the Word of God; then stand on the Word some more. Start reading the Word daily. Read ten pages a day for three weeks, and by the end of those three weeks, you won't even recognize yourself. You'll begin to see the life-giving flow come in and take effect in your body, your mind, and any physical circumstances you face.

It's the most glorious thing in the world. It's also the easiest thing in the world, but you must do your due diligence. Get in the Word and receive it with your heart, not your mind. Receiving God's Word from your heart will produce confidence in you.

 There's a confidence that comes with knowing God.

> Now this is the confidence that we have in Him, that if we ask anything according to His will, He hears us.
>
> —1 John 5:14 (NKJV)

When you don't have confidence in God, you end up thinking that your good Father is trying to abuse, neglect, and torment you with sickness and disease. You can't confidently fight against someone you think has good intentions for you. If you think God is your Father and He loves you, but He wants to beat the crap out of you with sickness and disease, you're left in a state of confusion. How can you be victorious over sickness and disease if you're in a state of confusion about who gave it to you? If you're confused about why you're going through what you're going through, it's because you don't have enough of the Word of God on the inside of you to decipher what's right from what's wrong.

The confidence you can have in Him comes from His Word. If you ask anything according to His will, it's yours. God's will is His Word.

When religious people deal with sickness and disease, they usually sound like this:

"I don't know if this is from the Lord, but if it be Your will to heal me, Lord, let it be done."

These are the words of someone who doesn't know what they're talking about. If you understand God's will, which is His Word, you understand that God is not the author of sickness and disease. When you understand He is not the author of sickness and disease, you don't pray those silly prayers.

The Bible says when you pray according to the will of God, He hears you.

That means to receive the answer to your prayer, you need to know God's will found in His Word.

And since we know He hears us when we make our requests, we also know that He will give us what we ask for.

—1 John 5:15

God will give you what you ask for when you understand His will for your life. If you lack that understanding, you can't expect your prayer to be answered. If you think it's God's will for you to be sick, you need to read your Bible.

The truth is, what you don't know has the power to kill you. Knowledge is, quite literally, power. That may be cliche, but it's accurate. God can't bless stupid. You can't believe incorrectly and expect God to defy His own laws and principles to answer your prayer.

Don't pray things like, "Father, if it be Your will that I am healed, then heal me. But if it's not Your will, show me why…" You don't have to wonder what God's will is; He wrote it down. All you have to do is read it, believe it, and receive it.

Many believers end up fighting the fact that healing is God's will for them. Don't be the type of Christian who prays for healing and then proceeds with chemotherapy and attempts to receive healing in their own strength with pills, physical therapy, herbs, and all types of remedies.

There's zero logic in taking matters into your own hands to get rid of sickness and disease while simultaneously believing that your disease is from God. If God is the one sending you sickness, why would you attempt to fight against it? Understanding what the Word of God says concerning His will is absolutely imperative for your healing.

GOD WANTS YOU HEALED

Some Christians read their Bibles every day and still lack the revelation of healing. They've completely missed it, and Covid-19 proved it. Too many Christians are afraid of sickness and disease. They don't really believe the full counsel of the Word. They don't really believe God is able to heal.

Too many people out there believe in their hearts and speak with their mouths that God put sickness on them. Entire denominations claim to be Christians yet believe God gives sickness and disease to teach you a lesson. *How insane!*

Let me be very clear. Any Christian who would try to get you to believe God has an inkling of desire for you to remain sick is a clown. If you've been indoctrinated to think that God is the one who brought sickness and disease into your life, this may sound strange to you. Let me be the first to tell you that what you've been taught is incorrect.

I will show you what the Word of God says about divine health and healing so that you can see it for yourself. I want you to receive freedom from whatever it is that's been put on your mind or body. I want you to be free from whatever has been tormenting you.

The first fundamental truth you must understand is that God does not want you to be sick.

 God wants you well.

I will take you through scriptures that indisputably prove it is not God's will for you to be sick. Not only that, but it's also God's desire that you would be healed and remain in divine health.

Let's begin with the Book of Matthew.

> Large crowds followed Jesus as he came down the mountainside. Suddenly, a man with leprosy approached him and knelt before him. "Lord," the man said, "if you are willing, you can heal me and make me clean." Jesus reached out and touched him. **"I am willing,"** he said. **"Be healed!"** And instantly the leprosy disappeared.
>
> —Matthew 8:1-3

Notice Jesus' response to the leper. "I am willing. Be healed!"

Jesus is willing, and because He was willing to heal the leper, He is also willing to heal you. *Why?* Because the Bible says that God is no respecter of persons (Acts 10:34). When Jesus answered the leper, He answered all of us. Jesus doesn't show favor to people based on their income or accomplishments. What He does for one, He does for all. God wants to heal your broken heart and He wants to heal your body.

I want you to know that God is a good God, and He loves you. We call Him Father. We serve a Godhead, three in one—God the Father, God the Son, and God the Holy Spirit. God the Father is a good Father. *Selah.*

Have you ever seen those St. Jude commercials? They film babies with oxygen tubes up their noses and premature bald heads. Do you then think, 'Yup, my God did that. He's sending cancer to these little babies.' If that's what goes through your mind, I'm sorry to say you have a mental disorder. If you think our good Father would send sickness and disease to teach you a lesson, or compassion, mercy, patience, or provide you an opportunity to share Jesus with the nurses in the hospital, I feel sorry for you.

I'm writing this for you so that you will know with certainty that you have the wrong mindset.

Not even an earthly father would cause their child severe pain under the guise of teaching them a lesson. How much less would our perfect, compassionate, and merciful Heavenly Father send us sickness and disease? God is sitting in Heaven wondering what is wrong with you for thinking that way.

Stop asking God to heal you. He's quite literally done everything He can do. He sent His Son to die on the cross to bring healing, forgiveness, and redemption. Then, He came back to Heaven and sent His Holy Spirit, who never leaves you and never forgets about you. He leads you into all truth.

Everything has been perfectly completed to give you access to freedom, forgiveness, redemption, healing, joy, peace, and salvation through Jesus, your elder brother. What else do you want Him to do?

GOD'S PLAN FOR YOU

There's nothing left for God to do, but there are things that every believer needs to do to receive from God. Understanding God's will is the only way to receive what He's promised you.

God's Word is His will. Anything you find in God's Word reveals His will for you. Based on this truth, we can confidently know that your health matters to God.

Receiving healing is a point of contention within the Body of Christ because, for most Christians, what they see and feel trumps what they believe and what the Word says. You may have heard nothing but negative reports about your health status up to this point. Maybe that's why you're in your present state. A state of darkness where you don't even have enough strength to look at your Bible.

If I've described your present situation, I want you to know there's hope for you even when the doctors have no answers or resolve for the issues you're facing in your mind and body. Jesus is the resolve.

He helped me. He set me free. He healed me. He delivered me. The attack on my life was two-pronged. It wasn't just physical. The enemy attacked my mind as well. Fear plagued me even after my body had begun to regenerate and I received healing. I was tormented in my mind because that's what bullies do–they linger.

It didn't matter how good I felt physically; it was as if I had this blanket draped over my head, and I was consumed by sorrow, fear, and anxiety. It was such an ugly time in my life that I literally lost the will to live. I was absolutely drained.

Then I cried out to the Lord, "If you set me free from this, I'll tell the world. I'll make it my life's mission to tell people how I gained this freedom." So here I am, fulfilling my promise to God by making it as clear as possible—healing belongs to you!

His plan for you also includes a long life.

> Joyful is the person who finds wisdom, the one who gains understanding. For wisdom is more profitable than silver, and her wages are better than gold. Wisdom is more precious than rubies; nothing you desire can compare with her. **She offers you long life in her right hand, and riches and honor in her left.**
>
> —Proverbs 3:13-16

The Bible's position on sickness and disease is clear. It doesn't just state God wants you healthy; He wants you to live a long life.

It's impossible to read the next 16 verses and make an argument against divine healing.

> Those who live in the shelter of the Most High will find rest in the shadow of the Almighty. This I declare about the Lord: He alone is my refuge, my place of safety; he is my God, and I trust him. **For he will rescue you from every trap and protect you from deadly disease.** He will cover you with his feathers. He will shelter you with his wings. His faithful promises are your armor and protection. Do not be afraid of the terrors of the night, nor the arrow that flies in the day. **Do not dread the disease that stalks in darkness, nor the disaster that strikes at midday. Though a thousand fall at your side, though ten thousand are dying around you, these evils will not touch you.** Just open your eyes, and see how the wicked are punished. If you make the Lord your refuge, if you make the Most High your shelter, no evil will conquer you; **no plague will come near your home. For he will order his angels to protect you wherever you go.** They will hold you up with their hands so you won't even hurt your foot on a stone. You will trample upon lions and cobras; you will crush fierce lions and serpents under your feet! The Lord says, "I will rescue those who love me. I will protect those who trust in my name. When they call on me, I will answer; I will be with them

in trouble. I will rescue and honor them. **I will reward them with a long life and give them my salvation.**"

—Psalm 91

It's God's plan for you to walk in divine health.

God created and executed a plan for your healing. He sacrificed His only Son and allowed Him to be brutalized so that by His stripes, you would be healed. He purchased healing for everyone who comes into covenant with Him. God didn't stop there. He also promised you vitality.

> **But you have made me as strong as a wild ox.** You have anointed me with the finest oil. My eyes have seen the downfall of my enemies; my ears have heard the defeat of my wicked opponents. **But the godly will flourish like palm trees and grow strong like the cedars of Lebanon.** For they are transplanted to the Lord's own house. They flourish in the courts of our God. **Even in old age they will still produce fruit; they will remain vital and green.**
>
> —Psalm 92:10-14

These Scriptures further demonstrate God's will and plan for your life. In contrast to God's plan, the American plan is to prepare you for retirement by age 50. Don't fall for that trap.

The Bible teaches that not only will you be alive, but you will also be fruitful in old age. In practical terms, that means this ministry will yield its greatest impact as I approach my 70s and 80s. That's when the greatest meetings should take place. You should have a plan that accounts for your continued and heightened success well into old age.

Webster defines health as "the state of an animal or living body in which the parts are sound, well organized, and which they all perform freely their natural functions." You need to understand what health is if you want to walk in perfect health.

God's plan is to have you walk whole and healed all the days of your life.

If you get this reality into your spirit, it will absolutely set you free. God's plan and purpose for you has always been that you would prosper and be in good health. He wants you sound in body, mind, and spirit. Everything in you should function as designed and be in perfect harmony.

To receive your healing, you have to claim it today. Don't put it off.

 Today is the day I receive my healing.

Faith is now. Hebrews 11:1 says, *"Now faith is…"* Faith is not yesterday or tomorrow; faith is this very present moment. You don't wait to receive your healing; you simply receive it as a free gift from God.

It's almost too easy for people to obtain. Jesus accounted not just for sin but also for healing, prosperity, joy, and peace. All these things were afforded to you because He died on the cross and poured out His blood for you.

By His stripes, you have already been made well.

GOD'S FORMULA

If you've already been healed by His stripes, why are so many believers still living with sickness and disease? It's because they haven't taken advantage of what belongs to them. You have to receive healing. Receiving is an action you have to take.

There's a formula found in the Word of God: Believe in your heart, confess with your mouth, and receive.

> But what does it say? "The word is near you, in your mouth and in your heart" (that is, the word of faith which we preach): that if you **confess with your mouth** the Lord Jesus and **believe in your heart** that God has raised Him from the dead, **you will be saved**. For with the heart one believes unto righteousness, and with the mouth confession is made unto salvation."
>
> —Romans 10:8-10 (NKJV)

Believe in your heart + Confess with your mouth + Receive = God's Promise.

The basic formula you use to receive your salvation is the same formula you use to receive everything from God. Take the same formula you used for salvation and use it toward your healing.

Think back to when you received salvation in your spirit with gladness. You had confidence in your salvation despite zero physical evidence to support what you knew in your spirit. That's the exact type of confidence and joy you need to receive your healing.

What you felt was faith coming alive on the inside of you to reaffirm your salvation. "No, I know I'm saved. I remember standing up there and accepting Jesus." Apply that same formula of faith to your healing. The Bible says,

> Is anyone among you sick? Let him call for the elders of the church, and let them pray over him, anointing him with oil in the name of the Lord. **And the prayer of faith will save the sick, and the Lord will raise him up.** And if he has committed sins, he will be forgiven.
>
> —James 5:14-15 (NKJV)

That's God's promise to you. All you need to do is understand and believe that what Jesus did for you didn't stop at salvation. Jesus carried out the complete work for your spirit, soul, *and* body on the cross.

God's formula of faith can be applied to all of God's promises. Believe, confess, receive, but you have to believe in your heart and not doubt.

> "I tell you the truth, you can say to this mountain, 'May you be lifted up and thrown into the sea,' and it will happen. **But you must really believe it will happen and have no doubt in your heart.** I tell you, you can pray for anything, and if you believe that you've received it, it will be yours."
>
> —Mark 11:23-24

Repetition is vitally important. When you're constantly in the Word, you're feeding your heart. So stick with what the Word of God says and receive your healing.

CONFESSION

Thank You, Lord, for Your Word. Thank You for revealing Your will to me. Thank You that it is Your will for me to be healed. Lord, I thank you that you have a plan for my life. A plan to prosper me and never to harm me, to give me a hope and a future. I receive my healing now. Not only that, I receive strength and vitality. I will live a long and productive life in Jesus' name, Amen!

QUESTIONS

1. Why do believers experience sickness, failure, and stagnation? _____
   _____

2. There's a confidence that comes with knowing God. Where does that confidence come from? _____

3. To receive the answer to your prayer, you need to know: _____
   _____

4. Why doesn't asking God to heal you make sense? _____
   _____

5. God's Word is His: _____

6. It's God's plan for you to: _____
   _____

7. Why is it unnecessary for you to wait to receive your healing? _____
   _____

8. God's formula of faith is _____ +
   _____ +
   _____ =
   _____ .

CHAPTER 2

SICKNESS IS SPIRITUAL

Jesus wasn't just wise when He walked the Earth; He *is* wisdom. People believe science has progressed to the point where it can explain sicknesses. Long gone are the days of old when people in the first century attributed many sicknesses to demons. However, people in the first century were closer to the truth than we are today. As science has progressed, people are the sickest they've ever been. New sicknesses continue to develop and evolve because sickness is spiritual.

Sickness is a spiritual thing.

It's not physical. Sickness may manifest itself physically, but its root is spiritual. Doctors and nurses will confirm that stress is the root of most diseases, including cancer. Stress isn't an entity in and of itself. Stress is simply fear. Stress is in your mind.

Doctors know chemotherapy can kill cancer cells and stifle their replication. What they can't tell you is where cancer cells come from or why they replicate and attack the body. What gives those cells life in the first place? They don't know. Doctors suggest stress and anxiety cause an imbalance in the brain that plays a role in the production of cancer cells. How do they fix the imbalance? They don't know.

I'm not bashing doctors. I'm pointing this out to illustrate that although we may have new technology and scientific names for sickness and disease in our current society, it doesn't change the fact that the cause of sickness and disease is spiritual. What you see in the natural realm is a reflection of what's happening in the spiritual realm. When something manifests in the natural realm, there is always a spiritual root to it because God is spirit.

When God spoke the Word, light existed, the firmament came into being, waters were created, and the animals came alive. However, before all those things came into existence, in the beginning was God's Spirit. The spiritual realm is more real than what you see in the natural realm because our natural realm can only produce what is done in the spirit realm. The world came into being because God spoke it into existence as spirit. When things manifest around you, whether it's a lack of peace, a broken marriage, or misbehaving children, there's always a spiritual root to those physical issues.

Racism is not the cause of America's problems. Any time there's hatred, it's a heart issue at the root. The only remedy is to know the love of Jesus Christ. He fills you with love and removes hatred. That means He removes racism and bitterness, and He fills people with His love, and then the atmosphere changes.

SICKNESS COMES FROM THE DEVIL

Let's be crystal clear. God does not give people cancer to teach them to appreciate life. You don't have to become sick to appreciate life. Jesus never offered religious platitudes to sick people. When people don't receive healing, they make allowances for their sickness. But this is anti-scriptural. Sickness is of the Devil.

John Alexander Dowie used to say, "Sickness is the foul offspring of its father, Satan, and its mother, sin." There was no sickness in the Garden of Eden. There won't be a children's hospital in Heaven. It's not part of God's plan for man to be sick. **You can know with conviction right now that God's plan for your life doesn't involve sickness and disease.**

God didn't plan for you to be sick. His plan is for you to be healed from all sickness and disease by His power and His Word. God didn't set aside a two-year period of your life for you to battle through a disease and have to cancel meetings to rest and recover. It's simply not part of His plan.

However, I'm positive it's part of the Devil's plan. The Word says to resist the Devil, and he will flee from you (James 4:7). The Word provides you with resistance to the Devil's plan.

> And you know that God anointed Jesus of Nazareth with the Holy Spirit and with power. Then Jesus went around doing good and **healing all who were oppressed by the devil,** for God was with him.
>
> —Acts 10:38

Every person Jesus healed was oppressed by the Devil. Sickness and disease are demonic. Again, in Luke 13, we see that Jesus attributed disease to Satan.

> One Sabbath day as Jesus was teaching in a synagogue, he saw a woman who had been crippled by an evil spirit. She had been bent double for eighteen years and was unable to stand up straight… "This dear woman, a daughter of Abraham, **has been held in bondage by Satan** for eighteen years. Isn't it right that she be released, even on the Sabbath?"
>
> —Luke 13:10-11, 16

To receive anything physically, it has to first be received spiritually. The Word of God is your weapon against the enemy, and make no mistake, you have an enemy. Your enemy wants to steal, kill, and destroy you. But if you have a firm foundation built on God's Word, your enemy can't touch you.

God is a good God, and the Devil is a bad Devil. Before we move any further, I need you to understand that.

The Bible says that things will grow worse until the coming of the Lord and Savior Jesus Christ (2 Timothy 3:1). You know who else knows this fact? *The Devil.*

It is his hatred for the children of God that drives him to attack your health. He knows his time is short. He desires to make your life as miserable as possible while he's still able to do so. But that doesn't have to be your reality.

There are two realms in the spirit: the heavenly realm and the demonic realm. Whatever is afflicting you is not coming from your Father in Heaven. There is only one source of darkness. There is only one source of sickness and disease. There's only one source of stagnancy and failure. It's the Devil.

> "The thief does not come except to steal, and to kill, and to destroy. I have come that they may have life, and that they may have it more abundantly."
>
> —John 10:10 (NKJV)

There's no place for sickness in an abundant life. As you read this, I pray every religious devil on you runs, now. Too many Christians have been trained to believe that happiness and Christianity cannot coexist. Many Christians walk around with a permanent frown because they think that's what it means to be spiritual. You may have been taught that it's not Godly to be a wealthy Christian. You may have been taught that wealth is of the world. I want you to understand that's not what the Bible says.

> For the love of money is the root of all evil...
>
> —1 Timothy 6:10 (KJV)

Notice the Word says the love of money, not money itself. In the same way that money doesn't make you evil, sickness and disease don't make you pious.

There are only two gates into your heart: your eyes and your ears. As we dive further into what God's Word says about His will for you, dust your Bible off and read it with your own eyes.

> And you know that God anointed Jesus of Nazareth with the Holy Spirit and with power.
> Then Jesus went around doing good and healing all who were **oppressed by the devil, for God was with him.**
>
> —Acts 10:38

There it is. God does not want you sick. I can't reemphasize this fact enough. Jesus views sickness as oppression from the Devil. God was with Jesus, and if He had been doing something out of line, God would have rebuked Jesus.

The above scripture provides a double emphasis. Jesus is God, but God the Father was *with* Him, which reveals that God's desire for His children is for them to be healed. Jesus healed all who were sick at the hands of the Devil. God the Father put His stamp of approval on what Jesus did. Jesus didn't go around doing good and healing all who were oppressed by God because God was teaching them a lesson. That's not what the Bible says. The Bible says Jesus went around doing good, healing *all* who were oppressed by the Devil.

As an aside, you have to be pretty marvelous to heal *all*, not some. Jesus didn't say, "You haven't paid your tithes. Take your leprosy and learn your lesson, idiot." Nope, that didn't happen. Jesus also didn't say, "I'll heal your child for now, but you haven't been at Bible study, so I'm going to give you a swollen ankle until you learn your lesson." Never happened. He healed ALL who were oppressed by the Devil. That is God's will, to heal all, because He's a good God.

The Devil is the one who oppresses people with sickness and disease. He is the father of lies. He is the coward of all cowards. When truth exposes a lie, the Devil runs and hides. So submit yourself to God, which is His Word, and expose the lies you've believed. The Devil will run from you.

Submission takes effort. Submission means denying yourself the privilege of trying to figure things out in your own strength and power. Refuse the urge to think about what the doctors have told you. Otherwise, in your mind, you're already dead. But if you submit yourself to God and His Word, something else takes over. It's no longer you who's in control. When you submit to God, He takes the lead. His Word takes the lead, and His Word says He healed all who were oppressed by the Devil. God, your Father, was right there with your elder brother, Jesus, approving it all.

LET'S TALK ABOUT JOB

People love to bring up Job when referring to sickness and disease, but God did not place sickness on Job. Don't bring up Job to make the false claim that God puts sickness on people. I can't count how many times I've heard people say things like:

"We don't know why God does these things…"

"The Lord gives, and the Lord takes away…"

How depressing!

There's a demonically inspired doctrine out there that has convinced people that God is the author of sickness and disease. It has persuaded people into believing that sometimes God takes away and sometimes God gives. Sometimes, God gives you a beautiful baby girl, and sometimes you give birth to a son and God takes him to Heaven. Yeah, that's what God wants to do, because apparently God is a schizophrenic in their minds. People actually believe this nonsense.

If you were to open the Book of Job, you'd understand that God came down and rebuked every single thing Job said about Him. Satan was the cause of Job's sickness. If Job went to see a doctor, he would have told Job his blood was inflamed and blistering on the skin. But there was a spiritual root to his sickness.

> So Satan left the Lord's presence, and he struck Job with terrible boils from head to foot.
>
> —Job 2:7

Most people don't realize that Job was one of the first books of the Bible ever written. Before there was an Old Testament, the Book of Job existed. The Book of Job isn't just about his afflictions. At the heart of it, the Book of Job is about him calling out to God for a mediator.

> I need someone to mediate between God and me, as a person mediates between friends.
>
> —Job 16:21

Job knew he couldn't approach God himself as a mere man; it would literally kill him. The purpose of the Book of Job was to reveal to us that humankind was in dire need of a Savior, a middleman. That's why God sent us Jesus. The Bible says that Jesus goes before the Father and intercedes for you (Romans 8:34). That was Job's desire.

You know what else happened in the Book of Job? God restored him **double**. Christians want to identify with Job and what he went through before he was rebuked by God, but they forget about what happened next. If you want to reference Job, you should have an expectation of double restoration, but no one talks about that. Why? *Religion.*

You can keep that. I don't want it, and neither should you. That's not what set me free. I know what it's like to be in a dark place, consumed with pain. To be in a place where doctors have no idea what's happening with you. They wish you the best and send you on your way because they have no idea what to do.

I know what it's like to feel like there's no end in sight. You're in pain, agony, darkness, and despair. You might be weary and fearful. You may have lost all will to live. That's what sickness and disease do to people. If you think for a second that God sent that to you, you're absolutely nuts!

DEVELOP A HATRED FOR SICKNESS AND DISEASE

Once you realize that sickness is of the Devil, you'll develop a proper hatred for sickness. My father, Tiff Shuttlesworth, says, "You'll never get delivered from a sin you're not disgusted with." You'll never be delivered from sickness and disease until you're disgusted with it.

John G. Lake said, "It's no more offensive for a man to be involved in adultery than it is for a man to be sick." Both adultery and sickness originate from Satan. Jesus redeemed man from both things, and neither of them has any place in the life of man.

If someone tried to introduce you to cocaine, you'd shun it. "No, I don't do that. I'm a Christian." You've had it ingrained in you from childhood: don't do drugs. But when you get an ear infection, your attitude is completely different. "Oh, I usually get them when the weather changes in the winter…"

You have a resistance to drug use because you know it's from the Devil. You know it's from Hell. You think sickness is a normal part of life, so not only do you put up with it, but you also make room for it. Some people think cocaine is a normal part of life, too. There are people who think adultery is a normal part of life. But as a child of God, you should have the same disgusted rejection for sickness as you do for sin.

> **Sickness does not belong in my body because sickness is of the Devil. Christ came to destroy the works of the Devil, and sickness has no place in my life.**

You pray differently when you hate something. When Peter's mother-in-law was very sick, Jesus rebuked the fever, and it left her (Luke 4:39). He addressed the fever as a personality. He spoke to it. He rebuked the spirit of infirmity. Jesus treated sickness and disease like an enemy all throughout the four gospels.

Jesus doesn't want you oppressed. He died for your freedom. His purpose in coming to Earth was so that you would be redeemed. Jesus' stance on sickness and disease wasn't passive; yours shouldn't be either. Too many people tolerate things in their lives. People become used to the mundane. People are so complacent the last thing they would think to do is stand up and fight. There's no desperation toward what the Word of God says concerning healing. There's no passion for walking in complete deliverance. Why tolerate sickness, disease, anxiety, or depression for years? You have to develop a hatred for what God hates, and God hates sickness and disease.

CONFESSION

Heavenly Father, I thank you that Your plan for my life doesn't involve sickness and disease. Your plan is for me to be healed from all sickness and disease by Your power and Your Word. I acknowledge that sickness is of the Devil, and I thank You that Your Word provides me with resistance to the Devil's plan. I rebuke sickness and disease. Sickness does not belong in my body because sickness is of the Devil. Christ came to destroy the works of the Devil, and sickness has no place in my life. I receive my healing today in the name of Jesus.

QUESTIONS

1. The cause of sickness and disease is: _____
_____

2. There are two realms: natural and spiritual. Which realm is more real? _____
_____

3. What has to happen before you can physically receive anything? _____
_____

4. Who is your enemy, and what is his purpose? _____
_____

5. How does Jesus view sickness? How do we know? _____
_____

6. You cannot reference Job without an expectation of: _____
_____

7. Complete the quote. "You'll never get _____
from a sin you're not_____with." — Tiff Shuttlesworth

8. As a child of God, you should have the same disgusted rejection for_____
as you do for _____.

CHAPTER 3

EVERY SPIRITUAL BLESSING—INCLUDING HEALING—BELONGS TO YOU

One thing people often miss regarding the things of God is what they already have in their possession. I can't tell you how often I've heard people pray, "Oh Lord, give me healing. Oh Lord, give me more faith." It sounds cute and spiritual, but it's not scriptural to ask God for either of those things.

When it comes to your healing, you need the full counsel of the Word. You don't need double or more of anything. God has already given you everything pertaining to life and godliness (2 Peter 1:3). He's given you all of Himself. He's given you the Holy Spirit. He promised to always be with you until the end of time (Matthew 28:20).

God has given you the fullness of Himself, but it won't manifest in your life unless you do your job. Your job is to yield to what's on the inside of you. First, you have to know what's inside you. Then, you have to yield to it.

It's impossible to make something work if you don't know it exists. I have a garage full of tools. My husband, Jonathan, has no idea they're in there. He's literally never picked up a screwdriver in his life. If something were to break in our house and I was not around, he would either go without it or wait for Amazon to ship a replacement. In reality, all he has to do is walk to the garage, pick up the screwdriver and two screws, and he'd be able to use whatever is broken.

He doesn't know the tools are accessible because he doesn't care about fixing things. It's of no interest to him whatsoever. He doesn't know he has the tools to fix what's not working properly, so he has to go without.

In the same vein, if you have no interest in what God's Word says about healing, then you have no understanding of what's already on the inside of you. The weapon, resource, and ability that you have isn't being utilized against the attack on your mind or body. It's as if you have a gun that you don't know is loaded. You don't attempt to use it to defend yourself against an intruder. You just let him take all your stuff.

You have to know what you possess. What *do* you possess? **Everything**.

 Everything pertaining to life and godliness belongs to you.

If you were to pray over your children's children 100 years from now, what would you pray? Many people might pray for healing, peace, or protection, but let's look at what Paul prayed.

> All praise to God, the Father of our Lord Jesus Christ, **who has blessed us with every spiritual blessing** in the heavenly realms because we are united with Christ. Even before he made the world, God loved us and chose us in Christ to be holy and without fault in his eyes.
>
> —Ephesians 1:3-4

Paul prayed that the church would understand what already belonged to them. That's what Paul prayed over them—understanding. He didn't ask God to bless them or give them houses and children. Nope. Paul's prayer illustrated what he believed to be the most important thing in the life of a believer—to be aware of what's already been given to you.

HEALING IS SPIRITUAL

Paul said we've **already** been blessed with **every** spiritual blessing. Spiritual gifts require a spiritual response. You are a spirit. You have a soul. You live in a body. Your soul is your mind, emotion, intellect, and will. Your soul is housed in a body. The real you is not your soul or your body. You are a spirit. When your body dies, you don't die. Your body will remain lifeless on Earth, and your spirit will go up to be with the Lord or down to Hell if you've never repented.

The spirit lives forever. Once you're born, you forever will be (Hebrews 9:27). God's method of healing is not through your physical body. When you read about Jesus' healing miracles, He didn't rub cream on people with leprosy. Jesus didn't practice acupuncture, He didn't inquire about supplements, and He showed no concern whatsoever for the condition of a person's body. Jesus healed through the spirit, and He continues to heal that way today.

What's in your spirit will manifest in your body.

The work Jesus did to redeem us was spiritual. He shed His blood. A doctor won't find a cancerous mass and shed his blood to make you better. God dealt with sickness differently than doctors because He knew the source of sickness was spiritual.

If I have back pain, I can take an Advil. But that's not addressing the root of the problem. My back pain might be caused by lack of movement, or because I've put on too much weight too quickly, or because I need to stretch. Whatever the cause may be, an Advil can't address it. Advil can only treat a symptom.

Jesus dealt with the actual root of sickness and disease. He didn't treat symptoms. The root is the Devil. I want you to comprehend that **receiving is a spiritual transaction**.

You received Christ through a spiritual transaction. A word was sent to you. That word was deposited into your spirit. God sent that word to you because God is His Word. That means God showed up and made a deposit, and you received it in your heart. At that moment, your heart trumped everything your mind was thinking. You chose to disregard your mind, and you received something by faith. You confessed with your mouth what you believed in your heart (Romans 10:8-10).

Have you ever noticed that when you're around angry people, you become angry? You don't even know why you're angry, but you feel yourself becoming increasingly impatient and annoyed. Maybe you were living a good life, and then you began to hang out with a group of busy-bodied women who drink all the time, and now everything is dramatic. You have all this Facebook and Instagram drama, and people hate your guts, and you can't understand why. You become like the people you hang around.

The same concept applies to the Word of God. If you surround yourself with the Word, it's reflected in the way you act, speak, and believe. When you first believed in your heart that Jesus is Lord and you confessed Him as Lord and Savior with your mouth so that you would be saved, did you see an immediate difference? You may have felt a difference because there's a freeing feeling that comes with knowing you're no longer in bondage. Any feelings of guilt and sadness may have left you. Although you couldn't immediately see it with your eyes, there was a real, tangible change on the inside of you.

> Therefore, if anyone is in Christ, he is a new creation; old things have passed away; behold, all things have become new.
>
> —2 Corinthians 5:17 (NKJV)

After you believed in your heart and confessed Jesus as Lord and Savior with your mouth, there was a change. *You became a new creature*. That change occurred, but you weren't aware of it at the time. You just knew you felt good. You still looked like you on the outside. You still thought like you, but a spiritual change took place.

The Bible says you were created anew. You were made squeaky clean. What happened on the inside of you slowly began to reflect on the outside as you began reading the Word and attending church. You began to hear and receive the Word of God with joy in your heart, and it began to change your mind. Then it changed the way you talked, and before you knew it, what happened on the inside of you took effect on the outside. The transformation that occurred on the inside of you became visible, but it wasn't made visible immediately. There was a process that had to take place.

> Now may the God of peace Himself sanctify you completely; and may your whole spirit, soul, and body be preserved blameless at the coming of our Lord Jesus Christ.
>
> —1 Thessalonians 5:23 (NKJV)

A perfection and sanctification process occurs through the cleansing and renewing power of the Word of God.

The change you undergo when you receive salvation doesn't happen in your soul or body; there is no physical change. You didn't turn blue upon receiving salvation. The change happened in your spirit. As your spirit slowly engaged in the process of sanctification, you began to gain an understanding of God's Word and will for your life, and subsequent change was made.

The next thing you knew, addiction fell off of you. Your mindset changed. You broke free from fear and anxiety. You may not be able to pinpoint how it happened; you just know it happened. All you did was simply receive salvation by faith and thank God for saving you. Then you became convinced of it.

That same conviction is what you need to have to receive your healing. It's no wonder people become frustrated after having hands laid on them. So often, people turn around and complain they're still in pain or feel the same. Then, they check in with their doctor to ensure everything is okay. "We have to use wisdom." What happens when "wisdom" says, "There's nothing we can do for you."? What happens when there's no medicine you can take for what you have? "Sorry, we hope you get it figured out because we don't know what to do. Best of luck." That's what I was told.

Many people have trouble understanding that what you receive in your spirit doesn't immediately come into effect in your body. Maybe the pain lingers. Maybe fear and doubt stick around longer than you expected.

If I cut a rose from a bush, it's still very pretty. It looks alive. It blooms, but that flower is dead. In a few days, maybe a week, you'll physically see it die. In a similar sense, I want you to come to the realization that when you pray and confess your healing and believe in your heart without a doubt, whatever is ailing you *has* to go. It has no choice.

You must receive it in your spirit and understand it doesn't matter what you feel. Your soul and body have nothing to do with what's happening in your spirit. Eventually, your body will catch up to the process of sanctification that's occurring in your spirit.

Let's look at Ephesians 1:3 again.

All praise to God, the Father of our Lord Jesus Christ, who has **blessed us with every spiritual blessing** *in the heavenly realms because* **we are united with Christ.**

If God has blessed you with every spiritual blessing, that means you lack nothing. If you have a problem in the natural, God has already given you the spiritual blessing to fix it. You don't fix your problems with your own strength and power. You simply receive the victory over your problem because it's yours. You activate it by faith. You simply say, "*It's done.*" You refuse to give the situation power. Refuse to allow it to keep you up at night. Refuse to fear it.

If the Bible says you're healed, why would you be afraid of dying? If God's Word says you have joy, why would you fear depression? It doesn't make any sense. If you're not convinced of what's on the inside of you, it gives way to this kind of double-mindedness. If you're not convinced yet, don't worry. You will be by the time you finish reading this book. You're going to see with your own eyes God has already given you every spiritual blessing in the heavenly realm. You have spiritual might on the inside of you!

We also learn from Paul's prayer that we are united with Christ. That realization of your unity with Christ is integral. If sickness, disease, anxiety, and depression can't defeat Jesus, then it can't defeat you because you're united with Him. The reason you have every spiritual blessing is because of your union with Christ Jesus. He's the one who gives you access to unlock the door to the blessings of Heaven. If you lack the awareness of your union with Christ, you think it's acceptable to allow sickness to fester. You think it's fine to accommodate anxiety.

Let's continue reading what Paul prayed over you.

> Even as [in His love] **He chose us** [actually picked us out for Himself as His own] in Christ **before the foundation of the world,** that we should be holy (consecrated and set apart for Him) and blameless in His sight, even above reproach, before Him in love.
>
> —Ephesians 1:4 (AMPC)

Before He made the world, He chose you. God loved you and chose you to be holy in Christ. You are without fault in His eyes. Even while you were still in sin, Christ died for you (Romans 5:8). Even when you were disgusting and filthy, Jesus looked down at you and said, "That's mine. You're my very own, and I've chosen you." Love did that.

FAITH FOR HEALING

> Now faith is the assurance (the confirmation, the title deed) of the things [we] hope for, being the proof of things [we] do not see and the conviction of their reality [faith perceiving as real fact what is not revealed to the senses].
>
> —Hebrews 11:1 (AMPC)

You were a walking dead man before you met Jesus. He brought you to life. The book of Genesis tells us that when Adam and Eve sinned against God, a death occurred.

God said in His Word,

> "but of the tree of the knowledge of good and evil you shall not eat, for in the day that you eat of it you shall surely die."
>
> —Genesis 2:17 (NKJV)

Did Adam and Eve drop dead in the garden? No, but a spiritual death occurred. Death didn't happen in the physical realm. It didn't affect their soul or body immediately. The immediate death that occurred happened to their spirit. It separated them from God.

God's entire purpose for creating humankind was so that He could show you love and have you love Him in return, of your own free will. He made you because He loves you. He created Adam and Eve, and the Devil came in and messed everything up. So God sent the second Adam, His Son, Jesus.

Jesus restored your fellowship with God by dying on the cross. The Bible says, He literally became sin and died on the cross for you. He didn't put on sin; He became it to restore your fellowship with God. He didn't only restore your fellowship with God, He restored your entire being—body, soul, and spirit.

Jesus died for all those reasons, but He also died so you would be healed. He also died so that you would have joy. He also died so that you would have peace. He became poor so that you would be rich. He left nothing undone. He left us with a beautiful gift, but there are elements of that precious gift that people refuse to open. Some will receive forgiveness of sin but not healing of sickness and disease. Not peace or joy. They have no knowledge of what belongs to them, even though Jesus died so they would have it.

The amplified version of Hebrews 11:1 says, *"faith perceiving as real fact what is not revealed to the senses."* Just because something is not yet revealed to your senses does not mean it's not present or taking place. If you have an understanding of salvation, this concept should be an easy one to understand. Hopefully, you're reading this because you understand that you received an unseen gift from God. When you received it, it impacted your words, thoughts, and actions. It's easy to apply this formula of receiving to your healing because you've already done it when you received salvation.

If you receive faith for healing in your spirit, it will manifest in your body. Just like when someone has an unclean spirit, it manifests in their body.

Faith for anything comes through hearing, including faith for healing. Once you've received the Word into your spirit, you speak the Word. That's why Jesus demanded verbal confirmation of faith before He healed.

"Do you believe that I can make you see?"

"Yes, Lord."

"What would you like me to do for you?"

"I want to receive my sight!"

Jesus required them to engage their faith to be healed.

In Mark 6, Jesus could not do mighty miracles because of their unbelief. That's the same reason so many people are sick today. The most neglected part of the American person is their spirit. You receive an education, you go to the gym, and you diet and take supplements. But most people do nothing for the part of them that affects things the most. The Bible is God's medicine for your physical body.

> My child, pay attention to what I say. Listen carefully to my words. Don't lose sight of them. Let them penetrate deep into your heart, **for they bring life to those who find them, and healing to their whole body.**
>
> —Proverbs 4:20-22

Through the hearing of the Word, you develop faith in your spirit. Then you begin to speak the Word, and your body follows the confession of your mouth through faith.

In Romans 4, Abraham believed those things spoken to him by God, and his body became strong, and he was empowered by faith. When you fill your spirit with God's Word, it will manifest peace, joy, strength, and divine health.

State what you want God to do for you today. As God's words enter into you, they give you strength, from the top of your head to the soles of your feet. Be healed, in Jesus' name.

Another example of faith in action in the spirit can be found in Matthew 21:19. Jesus saw the fig tree and cursed it because it bore no fruit.

In the book of Matthew, we see Jesus perform another healing miracle.

> When Jesus returned to Capernaum, a Roman officer came and pleaded with him, "Lord, my young servant lies in bed, paralyzed and in terrible pain." Jesus said, "I will come and heal him." But the officer said, "Lord, I am not worthy to have you come into my home. **Just say the word from where you are, and my servant will be healed.** I know this because I am under the authority of my superior officers, and I have authority over my soldiers. I only need to say, 'Go,' and they go, or 'Come,' and they come. And if I say to my slaves, 'Do this,' they do it." When Jesus heard this, he was amazed. Turning to those who were following him, he said, "I tell you the truth, I haven't seen faith like this in all Israel! And I tell you this, that many Gentiles will come from all over the world—from east and west—and sit down with Abraham, Isaac, and Jacob at the feast in the Kingdom of Heaven. But many Israelites—those for whom the Kingdom was prepared—will be thrown into outer darkness, where there will be weeping and gnashing of teeth." Then Jesus said to the Roman officer, "Go back home. **Because you believed, it has happened.**" And the young servant was healed that same hour.
>
> —Matthew 8:5-13

Because you have believed, it has happened. What you believe and what you speak is what you'll have. Jesus knew exactly what the Roman officer believed because he spoke authoritatively to Christ. He told Jesus to speak the word from where He was. *Faith speaks.* You have been given the faith to speak.

> But we continue to preach because we have the same kind of faith the psalmist had when he said, "I believed in God, so I spoke."
>
> —2 Corinthians 4:13

Real faith speaks. Anything in your life that doesn't bear fruit needs to be spoken to.

The pain you're in right now isn't producing fruit, so speak to it. Tell it to leave your life. Speak to it, just like Jesus spoke to the fig tree. When Jesus told the fig tree to wither up and die, the disciples marveled that the tree withered from the root. Jesus didn't understand why they were impressed. He basically said, *"This is nothing. You can say anything in My name, and it will be done"* (Matthew 21:21).

That's the power God's given you. You can speak what you believe, and you'll have it. That's why speaking what you believe is absolutely integral in seeing it come to pass. I want you to have enough faith on the inside of you to speak what you believe out of your mouth. Make up your mind right now. If something comes at you that doesn't align with God's plan of divine health, you're getting rid of it. Don't meditate on the symptoms. Don't make them yours by saying things like, "My arthritis, my back pain, my sinus infection…" Don't take ownership of sickness.

> For with the heart a person believes (adheres to, trusts in, and relies on Christ) and so is justified (declared righteous, acceptable to God), and **with the mouth he confesses (declares openly and speaks out freely his faith) and confirms [his] salvation**.
>
> —Romans 10:10 (AMPC)

It's upon your confession that things are solidified. It's not enough to just believe that Jesus died for your sickness. There has to be a conviction and a whole-hearted belief that what God did is for you. (Not the person next to you.) You can have knowledge and understanding of salvation, but until faith comes alive on the inside of you, you're not saved.

When you accepted Jesus as your Lord and Savior, the Bible says a measure of faith was given to you. **That means you have the faith to believe for your healing because you were given the faith for it by God.**

When you begin to listen to and read the Word, you'll develop an aversion for and resistance to anything that smells like sickness or disease. You have to hate sickness and disease to get rid of it.

There isn't a dire need for help in America and other first-world nations. You can kick your feet up and from the comfort of your own home, search your symptoms on WebMD, and Amazon the remedy right to your doorstep. You have to become desperate to receive healing God's way. Don't address sickness the way the world addresses it. Seek divine health. Shift your thinking from God *can heal* me to God *healed* me.

> "Saying, If you will diligently hearken to the voice of the Lord your God and will do what is right in His sight, and will listen to and obey His commandments and keep all His statutes, I will put none of the diseases upon you which I brought upon the Egyptians, for **I am the Lord Who heals you.**"
>
> —Exodus 15:26 (AMPC)

Notice that God didn't say, "I am the God who is going to heal you." He said, "*I am the God who heals you.*" God is a healer; that's who He is. He already devised a plan, and He already accomplished it on the cross. God's intention wasn't for you to need healing. He's already done what you need. Healing is a fundamental aspect of your walk with God.

> So let us stop going over the **basic** teachings about Christ again and again. Let us go on instead and become mature in our understanding. Surely we don't need to start again with the **fundamental** importance of repenting from evil deeds and placing our faith in God. You don't need further instruction about baptisms, **the laying on of hands**, the resurrection of the dead, and eternal judgment. And so, God willing, we will move forward to further understanding.
>
> —Hebrews 6:1-3

Grab a hold of this elementary principle. Healing is for today, and it's for you. Don't panic if you don't see something happen instantly.

> "And these signs will follow those who believe: In My name they will cast out demons; they will speak with new tongues; they will take up serpents; and if they drink anything deadly, it will by no means hurt them; they will lay hands on the sick, **and they will recover.**"
>
> —Mark 16:17, 18 (NKJV)

Things don't always happen instantly, although they can. Sometimes, there's a recovery process. It won't take 15 years, but there is progression. Don't allow the Devil to steal your belief and healing. Don't allow him to rob you of your peace. Shut the door on fear.

Divine health is one of the most precious things you can have. When you're sick and diseased, it's all-consuming. It's all you can think about. It lessens your capacity to think correctly. It becomes difficult to focus on your business, your children, your finances, or taking ground for the kingdom of God. It lessens your potential and ability to fulfill your purpose in life. Forget about the future, you're just hoping to make it to another day.

That's not God's plan. He wants you to be active and productive. When you contend for divine health, it's not just because you enjoy feeling good. There's a purpose behind it. The blood of Jesus has afforded every person who believes the precious gift of divine health.

What you say matters. Receive your healing, just like you did your salvation. Then, speak it out loud. If there's pain, tell the pain to go to Hell! *Buh-bye*. Don't tolerate pain. If it's a tumor, tell it to die. Jesus didn't talk to God about the fig tree or any sickness or disease; He spoke to the thing.

He said, *"Live,"* and Lazarus lived. He said, *"Be healed,"* and the sick were healed. You do the same. Every time you feel pain, speak to it.

Two things caused Jesus to marvel during His ministry on Earth. The first was when He arrived at His hometown and could only heal a few people because of their unbelief. He was amazed by their unbelief.

The second was great faith.

> "I know this because I am under the authority of my superior officers, and I have authority over my soldiers. I only need to say, 'Go,' and they go, or 'Come,' and they come. And if I say to my slaves, 'Do this,' they do it." When Jesus heard this, he was amazed. Turning to those who were following him, he said, **"I tell you the truth, I haven't seen faith like this in all Israel!** And I tell you this, that many Gentiles will come from all over the world—from east and west—and sit down with Abraham, Isaac, and Jacob at the feast in the Kingdom of Heaven."
>
> —Matthew 8:9-11

You have the capacity to make God marvel. Do you want it to be because of your great faith or your unbelief? Develop the kind of faith the centurion demonstrated. It's the faith you need to stand against sickness and disease.

All Jesus did was say, *"It's done,"* and it was done.

When you understand authority, you realize you already have dominion over sickness and disease. All dominion, power, strength, and authority has been given to you over every scheme of the Devil. **God has given you the authority to speak to sickness and disease, and it has to obey you.** That's how it works.

I want you to begin to speak to any disease or fear and command life to enter into your situation. Then, let the Word do the work while you rest.

 Faith rests. Faith doesn't test.

"Let me check my blood count." No! You didn't do that with salvation; you didn't wait to see a physical change to receive it. You received it by faith. Now, receive your healing by faith.

When Jesus taught His disciples about faith, He mentioned what you *say* three times and what you *believe* once.

> "For assuredly, I say to you, whoever **says** to this mountain, 'Be removed and be cast into the sea,' and does not doubt in his heart, but **believes** that those things he **says** will be done, he will have whatever he **says**. Therefore I say to you, whatever things you ask when you pray, believe that you receive them, and you will have them."
>
> —Mark 11:23-24 (NKJV)

You have to believe and speak first, and then you'll have what you desire. What you speak affects how you believe.

Dr. Mike Murdock says it this way, "Say the right words until the right feelings come." Most people let their feelings dictate the words they speak. "I know the Bible says that, but I'm poor." And you'll stay poor because you have a poor mindset. You hear the Word of God, and instead of using your mouth to amplify what God says, you use your mouth to override what God says.

Your mouth will be used to either amplify or override what God said.

About 20 percent of what I say when preaching isn't for the crowd; it's for me. I know I need to say what I want to see happen. What you believe and what you speak is powerful. What you say gets God's attention.

> So he began shouting, "Jesus, Son of David, have mercy on me!" "Be quiet!" the people in front yelled at him. But he only shouted louder, "Son of David, have mercy on me!"
>
> When Jesus heard him, he stopped and ordered that the man be brought to him. As the man came near, Jesus asked him, "What do you want me to do for you?" "Lord," he said, "I want to see!" And Jesus said, "All right, receive your sight! **Your faith has healed you.**" Instantly the man could see, and he followed Jesus, praising God. And all who saw it praised God, too.
>
> —Luke 18:38-43

Jesus said the man's faith is what healed him. How did Jesus know that man had faith to be healed? First, he referred to Him as *"Jesus, Son of David."* The Pharisees didn't believe that Jesus was the son of David. They believed Him to be a bastard son of Mary. They did not believe Mary became pregnant by the power of God. The way the blind man addressed Jesus made it clear that he believed Jesus to be the redemptive Messiah who had come to rescue His people.

When Jesus asked the man, *"What do you want me to do for you?"* he replied, *"I want to see!"* In effect, he was saying, "Have mercy on me! I believe you can do anything, and I want to see!" The words of faith the blind man spoke got God's attention.

Jesus isn't walking by your home or office today. But He's omnipresent and omniscient. What you say can either grab Him or repel Him.

YOUR COVENANT WITH GOD INCLUDES DIVINE HEALTH

If you're constantly in need of healing, there's a better way to live life. That better way of living is called divine health. God wants two things for you: He wants you to be financially stable, and He wants you to be in good health.

> Beloved, I pray that you may prosper in all things and be in health, just as your soul prospers.
>
> —3 John 1:2 (NKJV)

Notice, this scripture doesn't say He wants you healed; it says in health. There was no sickness or disease in the Garden of Eden. In the inception of what God established, there was never a need for healing. There was no remedy because it wasn't needed. Healing is the children's bread, and it is a daily blessing. The word says,

> No evil shall befall you, nor shall any plague come near your dwelling;
>
> —Psalm 91:10 (NKJV)

God's word doesn't just say He'll heal you. It says you won't need healing because disease won't come near your home in the first place!

> He shall call upon Me, and I will answer him; I will be with him in trouble; I will deliver him and honor him.
>
> —Psalm 91:15 (NKJV)

God will be with you in trouble. God actually likes trouble. He desires for you to come to Him whenever you find yourself in trouble. Your covenant with God carries the power to rescue you from ANY situation.

In Exodus 15, Moses and the Israelites went without water for three days. As they came to Marah, they finally found water, but it wasn't good to drink. When the Israelites complained to Moses, he took it to God, and the Lord instructed Moses to put the wood from a specific tree into the water, and it made it good to drink. Then the Lord said,

> If you diligently hearken to the voice of the Lord your God and will do what is right in His sight, and will listen to and obey His commandments and keep all His statutes, **I will put none of the diseases upon you which I brought upon the Egyptians, for I am the Lord who heals you.**
>
> —Exodus 15:26 (AMPC)

Take this literally. Egypt is a type of the world. **God promised you that none of the diseases that come on the world will come near you.** Rejoice and expect to be healed and in good health all the days of your life!

Again, in Exodus 23, God ensured the healing of His people.

> "So you shall serve the Lord your God, and He will bless your bread and your water. And I will take sickness away from the midst of you."
>
> —Exodus 23:25 (NKJV)

When you make a decision to serve God, He will take every sickness and disease out of your midst. If you need healing, you can expect to be healed. According to God's Word, if you don't need healing in your body, you can expect to remain free from sickness and disease for as long as you live.

God doesn't just heal; His name means Healer. Jehovah Raffa means *your physician*. He doesn't change. He was a healer in the Old Testament, He was a healer in the New Testament, and He is still a healer today.

> "If you diligently heed the voice of the Lord your God and do what is right in His sight, give ear to His commandments and keep all His statutes, **I will put none of the diseases on you which I have brought on the Egyptians. For I am the Lord who heals you.**"
>
> —Exodus 15:26 (NKJV)

God didn't just promise to heal you. He said He won't allow you to become sick.

> "So you shall serve the Lord your God, and He will bless your bread and your water. **And I will take sickness away from the midst of you.**"
>
> —Exodus 23:25 (NKJV)

In the same way He cleared the water in Marah, He will remove sickness from your life. You are the healed of God. From this day forward, the only time you step foot in a hospital is to pray someone out, in Jesus' name!

God made provision for healing in the Old Covenant.

We have a new covenant based on better promises. The following scriptures describe healing under the old covenant.

> He said, "If you will listen carefully to the voice of the Lord your God and do what is right in his sight, obeying his commands and keeping all his decrees, **then I will not make you suffer any of the diseases I sent on the Egyptians; for I am the Lord who heals you.**"
>
> —Exodus 15:26

> "You must serve only the Lord your God. If you do, I will bless you with food and water, **and I will protect you from illness.**"
>
> —Exodus 23:25

Notice, God didn't say He would heal you when you get sick. He said He'll protect you from illness.

> He also brought them out with silver and gold, and **there was none feeble among His tribes.**
>
> —Psalms 105:37 (NKJV)

The dictionary definition of feeble is "lacking physical strength, especially as a result of age or illness." The Bible says not one person in all the tribes who were in covenant with God was lacking strength as a result of illness. They were a perfectly healthy nation. Three million people and not one was weak, not even eighty and ninety year-olds. Why was no one weak? Because they were baptized in the cloud unto Moses. We have been baptized in water unto Christ. How much more do we have a right to divine health under the new covenant!

If God healed all His people under the old covenant, how can anyone say there's no more healing for us under the new covenant? That would effectively make our covenant worse than the old one. Do you think the Son of God left Heaven to give man a worse covenant than he had before? Of course not! Paul told us this covenant is more glorious in power and provision (2 Corinthians 3:6-15).

You may be wondering, if the new covenant is more glorious, why are so many Christians sick and oppressed? Dake's note on this passage of Scripture addresses this phenomenon perfectly.

"It is to the shame of the church to fall so far behind Israel in receiving promised benefits. Is it not logical that new covenant ministers and saints should meet the physical and spiritual qualifications of the old covenant? Is the old covenant the better of the two? Are its provisions and promises better? If so, then we should go back under the old covenant. What then, is wrong with the church that it does not get the superior blessing of the new covenant? Could it not be one because of unbelief? (Matthew 17:30, Hebrews11:6, James 1:5-8; 2) Because of widespread rebellion against such teaching, but surely it's not because God has lost His power or does not care to live up to His obligations made in the new covenant."[1]

Case closed.

When Christ enacted the new covenant, it was working well in the first century. In James 5, he had to ask, *"Is anyone even sick?"* Essentially, "I don't know if this even applies to anyone, but in case someone is sick, this is what you should do, and you'll be healed."

The only thing keeping the new covenant from appearing more glorious than the old is unbelief.

Jesus' purpose for coming to Earth was, in part, to take everything the Devil would ever use as an attempt to burden you. Christ took it, so you don't have to. He's already taken it and removed it. It doesn't belong to you.

> That evening many demon-possessed people were brought to Jesus. He cast out the evil spirits with a simple command, and he healed all the sick. This fulfilled the word of the Lord through the prophet Isaiah, who said, "He took our sicknesses and removed our diseases."
>
> —Matthew 8:16, 17

Jesus took your sickness and removed your disease.

Diabetes doesn't belong to you. Blood disorders don't belong to you. Heart disease and heart problems don't belong to you now, and you can refuse to make room for them in your 60s, 70s, and beyond. Jesus took ALL your diseases. The Bible doesn't say He will take, it says, *"He took."* He's already fulfilled his duty. Jesus, in His redemptive work, accomplished healing for your body.

Matthew 8:17 doesn't say, He'll heal you when you get sick. Jesus said you don't even have to become sick. You can be healed, stay healed, and dominate sickness and disease as a Christian. Healing is not just for apostles and evangelists. The Bible says everyone who believes can lay their hands on the sick, and they will be healed.

> "These miraculous signs will accompany those who believe: They will cast out demons in my name, and they will speak in new languages. They will be able to handle snakes with safety, and if they drink anything poisonous, it won't hurt them. **They will be able to place their hands on the sick, and they will be healed."**
>
> —Mark 16:17-18

Christianity that neglects to teach healing is not Christianity at all because healing is Christianity. Jesus didn't just heal; He *is* a healer. Any denomination that tells people to be like Christ but doesn't preach healing is like a golf instructor who tells his students to be like Tiger Woods, but not play golf. It's like telling someone to be like Jerry Seinfeld, but don't be funny. Christ is a healer. It's not something He did; it's who He is.

Maybe you're reading this and believe that God can heal you, but you don't understand why you haven't yet received healing. You need to understand the Bible basics of walking in the promises of God to walk in the freedom God has given you.

STRENGTH IN OLD AGE

Strength and vitality in old age are not the same as healing and a long life. Many people are alive and healed, but they're not strong. The Bible says that you will remain vital, even in old age.

> But the godly will flourish like palm trees **and grow strong like the cedars of Lebanon.** For they are transplanted to the Lord's own house. They flourish in the courts of our God. **Even in old age they will still produce fruit; they will remain vital and green.**
>
> —Psalm 92:12-14

You will flourish and bear fruit in old age if that's what you expect.

For surely there is an end; and thine expectation shall not be cut off.

—Proverbs 23:18 (KJV)

 Whatever you expect, you'll experience.

If you allow the world's norms to dictate how you see yourself, you'll get the world's results. If you visualize yourself weaker at sixty, or seventy, or eighty, that's what you'll experience. Remove every temptation to think of old age the way the world thinks of it. Toss your AARP magazines in the trash. Mute the prescription drug commercials. You don't need what they're selling. You will be strong in old age. Refuse to familiarize yourself with what people your age are suffering from. You have zero use for that information. You have the ability to grow stronger with age.

There are many examples of strength in old age throughout the Bible. Sarah couldn't have a child at 25, but she gave birth at 90 *and* nursed her child. Imagine how absolutely hysterical it would be to see a ninety-year-old woman nursing an infant in today's world. It would be funny now, and it was funny then. The Bible says, *"Sarah said, God has made me to laugh; and all who hear will laugh with me"* (Genesis 21:6).

At 85 years old, Caleb was able to travel and fight.

> And now, behold, the Lord has kept me alive, as He said, these forty-five years, ever since the Lord spoke this word to Moses while Israel wandered in the wilderness; and now, here I am this day, eighty-five years old. As yet I am as strong this day as on the day that Moses sent me; just as my strength was then, so now is my strength for war, both for going out and for coming in.
>
> —Joshua 14:10-11 (NKJV)

The Bible should shape your identity. If you base your identity on who the Bible says you are, you'll produce what God says you'll produce. You don't have to concede a single bodily function for as long as you live on Earth. You are not a money-making asset for the FDA or any pharmaceutical company.

I am (will be) strong and virile even in old age.

A LONG LIFE

God promised you a long life. There are several ways humans find themselves out of time on this Earth, and God ensured you protection from them in His word. Read Psalm 91 in its entirety, and see if you can come up with a single scheme of the Devil that can break through God's promise to protect you. You won't.

Here's are excerpts of your protections as a child of God.

*"…a thousand may fall at your side, and ten thousand at your right hand, **but it shall not come near you…**"*

"There shall no evil befall you, not any plague or calamity come near your tent…"

"For He will give His angels charge over you to accompany and defend and preserve you in all your ways…"

*"He shall call upon me and I will answer him; I will be with him in trouble, I will deliver him and honor him. **With long life will I satisfy him** and show him My salvation."*

"Long life belongs to you."

All of your covenant forefathers lived to be over one hundred years old. They were all under the old covenant. How much more will God protect you and give you a long life? You have a better covenant through the blood of Jesus. Expect God to give you what He said belongs to you.

YOU HAVE AN INHERITANCE

Did you know God has left you an inheritance?

> In Him we also were made [God's] heritage (portion) and we obtained an inheritance; for we had been foreordained (chosen and appointed beforehand) in accordance with His purpose, Who works out everything in agreement with the counsel and design of His [own] will,
>
> —Ephesians 1:11 (AMPC)

Your understanding of God's goodness shouldn't stop with salvation and Heaven. Your inheritance comes with a guarantee of the Holy Spirit. You have the fullness of God inside you.

> [For I always pray to] the God of our Lord Jesus Christ, the Father of glory, that He may grant you a spirit of wisdom and revelation [of insight into mysteries and secrets] in the [deep and intimate] knowledge of Him,
>
> —Ephesians 1:17 (AMPC)

Paul prayed that God would reveal Himself to you so that knowledge would give you access to what's already been given to you. You don't have to ask God to give you more faith, heal you, or anoint you. It's already in you. God has already given you everything. You lack nothing. God sent Jesus to die on the cross, and Jesus said, *"It is finished."* He left nothing undone.

God's not up in Heaven saying, "Oh shoot, I forgot about diabetes! If you've received this diagnosis, please see me separately." No! The restoration and deliverance of humankind is complete. Paul prayed that we would grasp it and fathom the kind of access we have.

Ultimately, you must be willing to enable God to move in your life. That requires you to yield. When you yield to God, you realize that you cannot do it on your own and with your strength and power. You release it and no longer allow it to affect your mind. You don't think about it. You're not under any pressure. There's no heaviness. When you decide to yield to the Holy Spirit, you completely surrender. You remove yourself from the equation and allow God to come in.

You have to realize that you have no idea how God will do what He's going to do. Your mind can't comprehend how the math will somehow transform a negative into abundance. You don't have to know. God doesn't need your help. He didn't need your help when He created the heavens and the Earth, and He doesn't need your help to rectify your situation.

Abandon your pride. Give no care to what others think. Solely focus on yielding to God. Faith is how you access what's already on the inside of you. You simply believe it's there. What you possess on the inside of you is not automatically activated. It has to be drawn out.

> "Therefore with joy will you draw water from the wells of salvation."
>
> —Isaiah 12:3 (AMPC)

There's a well on the inside of you that you need to activate and draw from. I want you to do something. We'll call it a homework assignment. Google the words "in you Bible" and read everything the Word of God says about what's inside of you. What's already in you will blow your mind. Knowing is half the battle. What you don't know has the power and potential to kill you.

> Which He exerted in Christ when He raised Him from the dead and seated Him at His [own] right hand in the heavenly [places], Far above all rule and authority and power and dominion and every name that is named [above every title that can be conferred], not only in this age and in this world, but also in the age and the world which are to come. And He has put all things under His feet and has appointed Him the universal and supreme Head of the church [a headship exercised throughout the church], Which is His body, the fullness of Him Who fills all in all [for in that body lives the full measure of Him Who makes everything complete, and Who fills everything everywhere with Himself].
>
> —Ephesians 1:20-23 (AMPC)

That's who you are. The same power that raised Jesus from the dead dwells in you. It quickens your mortal body. The fullness of God is in you.

CONFESSION

Heavenly Father, I thank You for giving me everything pertaining to life and godliness. Thank You for blessing me with every spiritual blessing. I receive healing in my spirit today. Thank You for sending Your Son so that I would have peace, joy, salvation, abundance, and divine health through the precious blood of Jesus. Anything that does not bear fruit in my life has to leave in Jesus' name! I rest in the revelation knowledge that I am healed today, from the top of my head to the soles of my feet. Thank You for the covenant you've made with me to keep me in divine health all the days of my life. I am strong, and I will live a long life. I thank You for the access You have given me as a child of God, and I yield to Your Holy Spirit now. I receive complete deliverance and restoration in the name of Jesus!

QUESTIONS

1. Why is it unnecessary and unscriptural to ask God to heal you? _____
_____

2. What was Paul's prayer for the church? _____
_____

3. You are a _____. You have a _____.
   You live in a _____.

4. How does healing manifest in your body? _____
_____

5. Anything in your life that doesn't bear fruit needs to be spoken to. What scripture supports this statement? _____

6. How do you know you have faith to be healed? _____
_____

7. What two things caused Jesus to marvel during His ministry on Earth? _____
_____

8. Your mouth will be used to either _____
   or _____ what God said.

9. What does God say about sickness and disease in the Old Covenant? (cite 3 scriptures)
_____

10. If healing is in the Old Covenant, and we have a New Covenant with better promises, why are so many Christians sick? _____

11. What happens when you yield to God? _____

CHAPTER 4

TAKE YOUR HEALING BY FORCE

A LACK OF KNOWLEDGE DESTROYS LIVES

God can't bless your ignorance. Meaning well and loving God does not translate into the activation of God's promises. It's like playing rugby without understanding the rules—everything looks ridiculous.

Why are a bunch of huge men without necks throwing a ball backward and hoisting each other into the air like ballerinas? Once my husband explained the rules to me, it made sense. I became intrigued by the game. Make no mistake, I don't have enough understanding to play the sport effectively. I would receive penalties left and right until I became disqualified.

Likewise, if you don't know there are rules and contingencies to the Word of God, you will continue to suffer. You will be disqualified from healing if you fail to understand what the Word of God says about it. You'll continue to take a passive stance. The definition of passive is *to suffer, not acting or capable of receiving*. The definition even states, *God is not in any respect, passive*. Let that sink in.

When I lost my son, I was told things like,

"Your testimony will bless so many people."

"This will catapult you into the next phase of your ministry."

"This will make you stronger."

That's a bunch of crap. I knew it then, and I know it all the more now. But why did it happen? So often, people struggle with why things happen. They think to themselves, "I'm a believer. I'm in the ministry. I preach against fear. What am I doing wrong? God must be teaching me a lesson."

People told me that my son would be full of disease, and God spared him the pain and took him to Heaven. That's not God. People mean well, but God doesn't operate that way. God was not the author of my son's death. People have a hard time understanding that God doesn't "call people home." They allow emotion to take over.

You already have all you need for life and godliness (2 Peter 1:3), and God is the same yesterday and forever (Hebrews 13:8). That makes you the variable, not God. The enemy is responsible for what happened to my family. The Devil does things he's not authorized to do because people are ignorant of what God's Word says belongs to them. He comes to steal, kill, and destroy, but God came to give you life more abundantly (John 10:10). It's easier to blame God for what happens than it is to come to the realization that it's a lack of knowledge that allowed the Devil to wreak havoc.

> "My people are destroyed for lack of knowledge,"
>
> —Hosea 4:6 (NKJV)

When Jesus speaks of faith to move a mountain, He's not referring to a physical mountain. You'll never need a physical mountain removed. Everything that needs to be removed from your life can be addressed with the knowledge and understanding found in God's Word. This revelation may not make you feel any better about past hardships. Join the club. But think how powerful and unstoppable you can be from this moment forward!

It's not the truth that sets you free; it's *knowing* the truth that sets you free. To know the truth is to be confident and certain. If you think for even a second that God allows you to be sick, there's a crack in your foundation. Once you conclude that what you allow on earth is what God allows and what you forbid on earth is what God forbids, you'll become unstoppable.

God can't move apart from you. The way you think and believe determines how God operates in your life. If you think God is a God of sickness and disease, you'll see that manifest in your life. The Devil will ensure your awful theology is evident in your life. The Devil loves poor doctrine. He will bend over backward to cater to anyone who believes God allows sickness and disease to teach His children a lesson.

As I dive deeper into the Word of God, I receive more and more revelation of what God's given us. It becomes increasingly apparent that He's given us *everything* we need. If you lack a breakthrough in any area of your life, there's a breakdown in understanding God's Word. Whether you're seeking healing, an increase in finances, a repaired marriage, whatever it is, God has equipped you with the answer. He's equipped you to be a problem solver.

You have everything you need to triumph over every force or demonic power. Nothing will by any means harm you. If you're still facing things that are causing you harm, realize that the problem is you.

Maybe you're not believing correctly, or maybe there's something you don't know. Your culpability is the only possibility because God has given you everything, including His will. His will is a plan of action for your life. Implement the wisdom God has given you in His Word in your everyday life. Then, when attacks come, you won't be shaken. You'll know exactly what to do.

Wisdom is simply the correct usage of what you know. There's no greater wisdom than the wisdom found in God's Word. Whenever you feel unsure of what to do, remember that as long as you know God's Word, you know what to do. If you don't know His Word, all you have to do is open it and begin reading. The Holy Spirit will help you and provide clarity when you seek Him.

The Spirit of God is the spirit of wisdom and revelation. Once He begins to help you, your understanding comes rapidly. It won't take you 15 years to find understanding. Too often, people grow weary before they even begin. They view reading their Bible as a daunting task. Don't buy into that lie. It only takes one prayer. Ask God to give you the wisdom and revelation that leads you into all truth. All of a sudden, things will begin to click.

Wisdom is not gained apart from the Bible. Wisdom doesn't come with age or education. It is the correct use of knowledge. Make the decision right now to never be passive in the things of God. If you're passive in small things, you'll respond the same way when something big comes along.

It can be tempting to succumb to a sore throat or a migraine and just grab some Advil and keep trucking along. That's the passive route. Stand against every pain. You have to do your due diligence.

In Mark 5:25-34, the woman with the issue of blood suffered for 12 years. When she heard about Jesus, the words He spoke ministered to her. The woman received the Word, and it built faith inside of her. Then she determined within herself that if she touched the hem of His garment, she would be healed.

Scholars believe that this woman was suffering from a sexually transmitted disease in a period when she could have been stoned to death for being unclean. Regardless of what people thought of her, regardless of the consequences, she risked her life for the opportunity to be healed. That's the kind of desperation you need to be set free. Tolerating sickness got her nowhere for 12 years. How long are you going to tolerate your sickness?

You may have poured a large amount of money into resolving your affliction and seen no improvement. What's the determination of your heart today? Your stance matters. Your aggressiveness matters in the kingdom of God.

> And from the days of John the Baptist until the present time, the kingdom of heaven has endured violent assault, **and violent men seize it by force** [as a precious prize—a share in the heavenly kingdom is sought with most ardent zeal and intense exertion].
>
> —Matthew 11:12 (AMPC)

You need violence on the inside of you to receive what God has promised you.

Jesus said, *"The works that I do, he will do also; and greater works than these he will do…"* (John 14:12). What did Jesus do? He went about healing all who were oppressed by the Devil. Healing is in your DNA. You don't have to be the Devil's punching bag. You can stand against the enemy.

The Devil wants you to be so ignorant of God's Word that you continue to blame God for your sickness. God has equipped every believer with the power and ability to do something about sickness, disease, and every type of evil happening in the world. You can't blame God for what happens on earth.

Religion is an ugly thing. It causes people to use God's sovereignty as an excuse to be weak and defeated. In reality, the truth of God's Word causes you to walk in power and dominion. Religion leaves you passive. It causes you to believe that God will do whatever needs to be done. God will save the country. How foolish! God has no hands except for our hands, no mouth except our mouth, and no feet except our feet. God uses yielded vessels. He uses individuals created in His image to share His message. If you understand His Word and are willing to act on it, He'll use you.

The Bible is full of stories about individuals who understood God's Word. David, Moses, Abraham, Esther, and Daniel. Each one acted independently. God didn't assemble an all-star team. All He needed was a single person to carry out His will. These men and women of God were aggressive and violent toward the things of God.

God doesn't back passivity. Passive means "unresisting, not opposing, suffering without resistance." God didn't give you power, dominion, and authority so that you could yield to dialysis, chemotherapy, and allergy medication.

 Don't make room for sickness. Stand and fight for your right to be healed!

God says in His Word, *"Oh, that you would choose life that you and your descendants might live!"* (Deuteronomy 30:19). That means you can also choose death. This Scripture reveals that the decision is bigger than what happens to you. Choosing life affects your children and grandchildren. It shapes your legacy.

At age 15, my sister and I were the only ones in our family to receive salvation. That decision to serve God impacted my entire family. It resulted in my mom, dad, sisters, brother, nieces, and nephews all loving and serving the Lord. If my sister and I failed to make that decision at such a pivotal age, I don't even want to think about the potential state of my family. I stuck with God, and now I can see and experience the beautiful harvest it produced.

The decision is completely up to you. You can stand firm in God's Word or fail to make that decision and fold under the first sign of pressure; either way, it will affect your family.

All you have to do from this moment forward is choose to believe the Word. Choose to be aggressive and violent when it comes to what God has promised you. Refuse to allow fear to infiltrate your mind.

Jesus was given the name above every name. If what you're suffering from has a name, it has to bow to the name of Jesus. It doesn't matter if that name is diabetes, fibromyalgia, or multiple sclerosis; it all has to bow.

Be violent about your healing, just like the woman with the issue of blood who gave no care to what people did to her. *Are you there yet?* If not, keep working, keep reading, and keep studying. You can develop your faith in God's Word to the point where it becomes second nature. It will no longer be second nature for you to grab that bottle of Advil when you feel an attack come on your body. Your new second nature will be to speak to the pain and tell it to go back to Hell.

You can walk in dominion and strength all the days of your life. There's no sickness in heaven. There's no disease, anxiety, depression, or lack in Heaven. You can have heaven on earth (Matthew 6:10).

CONFESSION

I refuse to be passive any longer. From this moment forward, Holy Spirit bring every passive instinct to my attention. Help me to realize everything I've been tolerating. Every passive tendency in me has been replaced with fierce tenacity and aggressiveness. I am violent toward the things God has promised me in His Word. Thank You, Father, for giving me all the power, dominion, and authority over sickness and disease.

QUESTIONS

1. Everything that needs to be removed from your life can be addressed with: _____
_____

2. How is the Devil able to do things he's not authorized to do? _____
_____

3. What can you do to ensure you won't be shaken when attacks come against you? ____
_____

4. Define wisdom: _____

5. Religion leaves you passive; what does the truth of God's Word produce?_____
_____

6. If what you're suffering from has a name, it must do what? _____
_____

CHAPTER 5

SEVEN HINDRANCES TO DIVINE HEALING

Although healing belongs to you, the Devil will take every opportunity to illegally access your body.

1. PRIDE

Many Christians are sick but refuse to receive prayer. That's not scriptural. The Bible says,

> Is anyone among you sick? Let him call for the elders of the church, and let them pray over him, anointing him with oil in the name of the Lord. And the prayer of faith will save the sick, and the Lord will raise him up. And if he has committed sins, he will be forgiven. Confess your trespasses to one another, and pray for one another, that you may be healed. The effective, fervent prayer of a righteous man avails much.
>
> —James 5:14-16 (NKJV)

It doesn't matter who you are. You could be a pastor, evangelist, preacher's wife, or involved in full-time ministry. The Bible says if you're sick, have hands laid on you in prayer.

Don't let pride get in the way of this instruction. Humans tend to think, "I got this; I can figure it out."

> Pride goes before destruction, and a haughty spirit before a fall.
>
> —Proverbs 16:18 (NKJV)

Eventually, you'll come to a point where you can't figure it out on your own. You don't have to wait until you reach that point. You can accept the fact that every human on earth needs help. You need God to intervene.

 If you want Him to intervene on your behalf, you must obey His Word.

Pride affects your productivity as a believer. Pride will interfere with your ability and willingness to witness to people. It will impede your giving. It will prevent you from getting prayer. Many Christians convince themselves they deserve sickness. If you're one of those people, let me ask you something. Are you above what the Word of God declares over your life? *No.* It's pride that's caused you to come to that conclusion.

"I know the Word of God says that, but my case is really rare..." *You do not deserve sickness.* You are not the exception. God makes no exceptions in His Word for sickness.

2. WICKEDNESS

Many people don't realize you can be a Christian and still have wickedness in your life. You can say the prayer of salvation, attend church on Sundays and Wednesdays, and still have things in your life that don't resemble Jesus. There are times when I've had to reel myself in. I'd love to tell some idiot in the comments what I really think sometimes, but I can't because I'm righteous. That means I must let go of the evil desire to engage in what my flesh feels like doing.

Evil is all around us, and it's easy to engage in. So, get off your high horse if you think this doesn't apply to you. People speak evil of their pastor, co-workers, or even their own family members.

The Bible says that to obtain a long life, you have to keep your tongue from speaking evil.

> Does anyone want to live a life that is long and prosperous? Then keep your tongue from speaking evil and your lips from telling lies! Turn away from evil and do good. Search for peace, and work to maintain it.
>
> —Psalm 34:12-14

If you've developed a momentum for doing evil your entire life, it feels natural for you to lie or engage in wicked things. Once you become saved, it's easy for you to continue in the same momentum. It takes intentionality to remove yourself from that track and move toward the goodness and righteousness of God. It's made possible only by His Word.

Sadly, many Christians don't even know what they're doing is wrong because they don't read the Word. If you don't read the Word and no one tells you what you're doing is evil, it's no surprise that you don't live a righteous life. Wickedness in your life is a barrier to healing and divine health.

 Read God's Word and learn to identify any area of your life that doesn't align with it.

3. BITTERNESS

Let go of unforgiveness and hatred. It's not okay to hate gay people or someone of another race. It's also not okay to hate politicians. You can hate sin and wickedness, but you cannot hate individuals.

> Look after each other so that none of you fails to receive the grace of God. Watch out that no poisonous root of bitterness grows up to trouble you, corrupting many.
>
> —Hebrews 12:15

It's possible to lose the grace of God in your life. Grace is vitally important to complete what you've been called to do. You need grace for your body, your mind, your finances, and your relationships.

 The poisonous root of bitterness can cause you to lose the grace of God.

The poisonous root of bitterness will literally kill you. Hatred and bitterness are a physical poison to your body. Unforgiveness has a spiritual root.

If you still have unforgiveness toward the person who raped you, or a hard heart toward your father who left you as a child, or you're still carrying a hurt heart because a minister hurt your feelings, you need to let it go. Understand that if you have a hard heart toward people, you have a hard heart toward God.

> If we love our brothers and sisters who are believers, it proves that we have passed from death to life. But a person who has no love is still dead. Anyone who hates another brother or sister is really a murderer at heart. And you know that murderers don't have eternal life within them.
>
> —1 John 3:14, 15

Anyone who hates a brother or sister is a murderer at heart. Not only do you not have eternal life, but when you die, there will be judgment against you. If you forgive those who've sinned against you, your heavenly Father will forgive you, but if you don't, you'll reap judgment (Matthew 6:14-15).

 Harboring unforgiveness in your heart will not only prevent you from receiving your healing, but it will also keep you from entering Heaven.

You're not saved. By faith, you receive salvation; by faith, you receive forgiveness; and by faith, you need to forgive. You don't have to call anyone and let them know you forgive them. You just have to ask your heavenly Father to forgive you for holding a grudge.

Confess to Him that you forgive them. Release it out of your mouth today, and watch healing come quickly.

There is a spiritual root to the attack in your life. It's not Billy or Sharon spearheading the attack. An underlying enemy sent them to take you off course to cause you to die before your time from sickness and disease. It's the plan of the enemy to get you so bitter that you stop attending church and quit believing in God. Make the choice to let go of the hatred and bitterness and decide to cling to the love that God has given you.

> We know how much God loves us, and we have put our trust in his love. God is love, and all who live in love live in God, and God lives in them.
>
> —1 John 4:16

When you choose to walk in love, there is a manifestation of God's power in your life. It's not always the easiest thing to do, but it's the best. I don't know about you, but I don't want to go to Hell. That should motivate you to walk in love. I'll never do anything that's going to be offensive to God. Choosing to live in love and refusing to hate will enable you to abide in love.

4. ANGER

Anger is a footstool for the enemy. Ecclesiastes 7:9 says to *"Control your temper, for anger labels you a fool."* Foolishness cuts your life short (Ecclesiastes 7:17).

I had an anger problem for several years, even after being saved. I would manifest with my fists, with rage, with yelling and slamming things. Every time it happened, I would feel a presence of evil swoop in. It was difficult for me to break free from that.

Anger is an overreaction to the errors of others. Relax. God has given you fruits of the Spirit. You have gentleness, patience, and long-suffering. The Bible says to make room for people's errors (Colossians 3:13). People will fail you. They will say things they shouldn't say, even your own family. Who cares?!

Shut the door on anger. Control your temper. Don't allow the enemy to come in. Anger will lead you to die before your time.

We used to do prison visitations. I still remember this huge inmate. He must have been 6'4". He was a monster of a man, but he had the kindest face. I would see him in jail worshiping the Lord. I could see God ministering to him. I would think to myself, I hope he's one of the ones who's getting out soon.

The jail we visited had two types of prisoners: the ones who were in for misdemeanors and would be let out in months, and the ones who were in holding until they could be transferred to larger prisons where they would serve serious time.

I was hoping this guy would be released soon. To my surprise, I found out he burned his girlfriend alive in a vehicle because he caught her cheating. He blacked out in anger, and the only thing he can remember is seeing the car engulfed in flames.

He's in prison for the rest of his life. Most people in jail for murder aren't really murderers. They're people who overreacted in a moment of fear, insecurity or hurt.

 Anger opens the door for the enemy to come in and destroy your life in a moment of weakness.

5. NO REST

God took a day to rest. Rest is scriptural. God produced in six days, and on the seventh day, He rested and called it the Sabbath. Whether you're a mother, a business owner, or a minister, you must have a day of rest. That may look like not doing laundry, ordering out, kicking up your legs, going to the playground with the kids, and enjoying yourselves. Detach from the world. People in the Body of Christ don't rest, especially ministers.

> Meanwhile, I thought I should send Epaphroditus back to you. He is a true brother, co-worker, and fellow soldier. And he was your messenger to help me in my need. I am sending him because he has been longing to see you, and he was very distressed that you heard he was ill. **And he certainly was ill; in fact, he almost died.** But God had mercy on him—and also on me, so that I would not have one sorrow after another. So I am all the more anxious to send him back to you, for I know you will be glad to see him, and then I will not be so worried about you. Welcome him in the Lord's love and with great joy, and give him the honor that people like him deserve. **For he risked his life for the work of Christ, and he was at the point of death while doing for me what you couldn't do from far away."**
>
> —Philippians 2:25-30

For the work of Christ, Epaphroditus came close to death. He risked his life. You need to have regard for your life. Take meaningful time to spend with your family.

My family takes a very proactive approach to spending quality time together. Our schedules are crazy, but it's not an excuse to neglect rest and quality time.

What makes you think you can do it better than God? God needed rest, and so do you.

6. NO JOY

If you want your healing or anything else that was afforded to you through salvation by the blood of Jesus at Calvary, it starts with joy.

And Nehemiah continued,

> "Go and celebrate with a feast of rich foods and sweet drinks, and share gifts of food with people who have nothing prepared. This is a sacred day before our Lord. Don't be dejected and sad, for the joy of the Lord is your strength!"
>
> —Nehemiah 8:10

> "See, God has come to save me. I will trust in him and not be afraid. The Lord God is my strength and my song; he has given me victory." With joy you will drink deeply from the fountain of salvation!
>
> —Isaiah 12:2-3

> A merry heart does good, like medicine, But a broken spirit dries the bones.
>
> —Proverbs 17:22 (NKJV)

There's something about joy and laughter that fights depression. If you want to come out of the situation you're in, you must joy your way out. I'm using joy as a verb. Just like you put on shoes or a garment to clothe your nakedness, you need to put on joy every day of your life to maintain health and receive your healing.

Healing doesn't come through your tears, sadness, or despair. There's strength and joy in God's presence. If God is not in your midst, there will be an absence of joy. You have to contend for joy. You have to put on joy to receive peace and healing.

 You must actively pursue joy.

If you don't have a joyful heart, you'll have a broken spirit. A broken spirit literally dries up your bones. A broken spirit leaves you brittle and weak.

I was in such despair and sadness at the loss of my son that I had a pity party for myself. "I'm sick. I had surgery. I'm on too many medications. I can't get comfortable." I had to decide to be in joy.

Rejoice, and again I say rejoice! (Philippians 4:4). If you're having difficulty finding joy, start with gratitude. Think about all the good things. For me, it looked like this:

"Thank you that I'm alive because I could have died. You kept me from dying because you have a purpose and a plan for me. Thank you for seeing the purpose and potential you put in me, and for seeing me through. Your hand wasn't the cause of what happened to me, but thank you for your mercy."

Then, I turned on the show *Impractical Jokers*. I'm not suggesting you do this. But it was on, I couldn't find the remote, and I couldn't move. The show made me chuckle. I couldn't laugh at the time.

I know firsthand that when you're in a time of loss and pain, it becomes all-consuming. It sucks. There's no other way to describe it. I'm sorry you're going through what you're going through right now, but the only way out is to have joy. Start wherever you can. Put on a movie you know is going to make you laugh. Medicine from the doctor can't solve everything.

A cheerful heart has medicinal effects that will heal your broken heart and heal your body.

If you've reached the point where you've lost hope, you've probably lost joy too. Get your joy back, and your hope will return. Joy is the only way to receive your healing today. Laugh. Do it now! Joy pacifies fear. Joy pacifies sadness and depression. If you don't get rid of those things, they'll take the fight right out of you. Find a way to joy. Put on joy every day of your life.

7. NO REGARD FOR YOUR OWN HEALTH

In a previous point, we read that Epaphroditus worked himself to the point of illness for the Lord. You have to have regard for your own life, and that includes your health. If you have no regard for what you eat or your daily activity, you might as well plan your death.

When Jesus was tempted in the wilderness, Satan told Jesus to throw himself off a ledge and have the angels save Him. Jesus refused to tempt the Lord. You don't tempt the Lord by doing things you know are wrong and then expect God to save you. Jesus knew that throwing Himself off a building in an attempt to move the hand of God was stupid. Yet here we are, especially Americans, sucking down high fructose corn syrup and sugar like it's medicine. Sugar is correlated with diabetes, tumors, and obesity. Your eating and drinking habits are an indication of the regard you have for your life.

Not everything in the Garden of Eden was approved by God to eat. Likewise, not everything made by man should be approved to enter your body. Studies have found a correlation between diet drinks and cancer, as well as Alzheimer's. The Bible says that you will be judged if you don't judge yourself.

Take an evaluation of what you're doing with your life. Have you moved? How many steps have you taken today? When was the last time you worked out? When was the last time you had a salad? Are you grabbing Taco Bell night after night? There's no one-size-fits-all formula for health, but you must have regard for your health.

I used to suck down 3 to 4 ice-cold Red Bulls a day. I remember one morning, I went to buy another Red Bull at 7/11, and the Holy Spirit said, "Don't touch it again." I thought to myself, 'No way.' I ignored it, and I suffered the consequences. I began getting dizzy spells and heart palpitations, and I wondered what could be causing them. Then suddenly, the Holy Spirit reminded me that I was still downing Red Bulls after He told me to stop.

It's not a lack of faith to read the ingredients label, especially in the world we live in today.

If you expect to be healed and walk in divine health, you must learn to self-evaluate and ensure that you are not engaging in anything that will hinder your God-given right to healing.

CONFESSION

Heavenly Father, thank You for divine healing and for sending Your Holy Spirit to live inside of me to convict me of any hindrances to your healing power. From today, I give no place to pride, wickedness, bitterness, and anger. I will actively pursue joy every day of my life. I will rest when my body needs rest, and I will hold my life in high regard.

QUESTIONS

1. According to the Bible, what must you do if you are sick?_____
_____

2. If you want God to intervene on your behalf, what must you do? _____
_____

3. The Bible says to _____ to obtain a long life.

4. Bitterness can cause you to lose: _____
_____

5. Walking in love causes: _____

6. _____ is an overreaction to the actions of others.

7. Anger opens the door for the enemy to: _____
_____

8. God produced the world in six days. What did He do on the seventh day? _____
_____

9. To receive peace and healing, what do you have to put on? _____
_____

10. If you're having difficulty finding joy, what can you do? _____
_____

11. What do your eating and drinking habits indicate? _____
_____

CHAPTER 6

HOW TO COOPERATE WITH GOD FOR HEALING AND A LONG LIFE

The ability to appropriately blend Scripture with health is rare. Most people either completely abandon divine healing and place all their faith and trust in holistic remedies like berries and detoxes, or they focus solely on God's ability to heal while completely ignoring God's instructions for remaining in good health. This chapter will blend the two previews with appropriate balance.

Divine health is a cooperative effort between you and God. Jesus didn't heal people by correcting their diet. Jesus didn't suggest that the blind man eat more carrots. He didn't instruct the cripple man to remove inflammatory foods from his diet. Divine healing comes from the power of God. But after God heals you, you have a part to play to remain in good health.

When Jesus raised Jairus' daughter from the dead, the first instruction He gave was for her to eat. He recognized the need for nourishment after He healed her physical body.

We are no longer under the law. However, it does provide us with some insight. In God's covenant with His children, He promised to keep them well, but He also gave them instructions on what to eat and what not to eat.

If you weigh 400 lbs. and have heart disease, it's not the Devil attacking you. I don't say this to condemn you. I'm broaching this topic to help you attain the health, strength, long life, and fruitfulness that God afforded you. Diet is no substitute for divine healing.

However, after you've been healed, cooperation with God's instructions is required to maintain good health.

If you were a four-pack-a-day smoker, God will heal you of COPD because He's a merciful God. But after you've been healed, you need to recognize the actions that allowed the disease to enter your life and stop.

As you continue reading, I will introduce 14 points to consider. Some require you to take action to bring you into alignment with God's plan for divine health.

1. DO YOU HAVE A FOOD ADDICTION?

Generally speaking, humankind has always had difficulty handling excess. If you live in America, the chances are you don't have to pray for food. Your next meal doesn't require an act of faith. However, in many countries around the world, that is a reality.

If you're reading this, it's likely your concern is not *if* you will be able to eat but *what* you will decide to eat. You have millions of options when choosing what to eat and drink. If you don't handle those options appropriately, they can easily lead to obesity. When you combine a sedentary lifestyle with a poor diet, you're on a fast track to obesity.

When Jesus told the crippled man to be healed, He later told him,

> "Now you are well; so stop sinning, or something even worse may happen to you."
>
> —John 5:14

You can be healed by God and still see disease return to you unless you turn from your sin. The Bible tells us gluttony is a sin. Let me be clear. I'm not skinny because I live on a higher health plane than most people. I am genetically built this way. I used to have to eat when I wasn't even hungry just to remain the same weight. That doesn't mean I haven't had to take action to keep myself in good health.

Food addiction is a real thing. I've encountered people who act like they're going through literal drug withdrawals when they don't eat at the same time every day. I've been in meetings with people who become completely distracted as soon as food arrives. They have tunnel vision for food. Do you freak out if you haven't eaten for a few hours? If this sounds familiar, food addiction is not a far-fetched conclusion.

Food shouldn't have control over you. Nothing should be your master except Jesus. I fast because the Bible teaches it, but fasting comes with an added benefit. The potential control that food can have over you is broken when you fast.

The Bible places gluttony right next to drunkenness. It's an abuse of your body. A diagnosis is required before the remedy can be prescribed. You can't operate in gluttony and expect to live a long, healthy life.

It's uncommon to see a 375 lb. eighty-five-year-old. Why? Because a sedentary lifestyle coupled with obesity is a killer. Once you've received healing, you must take your life seriously and stop abusing your body with food. It will take effort.

America is designed for you to be obese. Even salads, a food synonymous with health, are over-portioned. You may order a salad thinking you're making a healthy choice, but once the restaurant adds dressing, croutons, and cheese to it, you might as well have had a cheeseburger. Eating healthy in America requires restraint.

If you have difficulty saying no to food or going without eating for a few hours, you need to ask the Lord to help you get your food addiction under control.

2. UNDERSTAND THE CONNECTION BETWEEN THE FDA AND THE PHARMACEUTICAL INDUSTRY

As an American, you live in a country with very little interest in helping you eat healthy. Think about the long-published and USDA/FDA/DOA-endorsed food pyramid that suggests Americans eat primarily carbohydrates with very little meat to be "healthy." Through experience and science, we now know that this is the opposite of "being healthy." The same entity that regulates food also controls the drugs. The FDA and the USDA are the federal agencies that "approve" and "allow" ingredients in your food. These are the same agencies that "approve" and "allow" all the drugs into the market to "cure" you of the diseases caused by the ingredients "allowed" and "approved" to be in your food.

One quick look at the ingredients on the back of your food packages will horrify you—it's one unrecognizable ingredient after another. If the ingredients our federal government agencies allow in bread alone were found in bread sold at any European bakery, it would result in a hefty fine and, most likely, a jail sentence.[1]

In America, 70 percent of people regularly take prescription drugs.[2] The love of money is the root of all evil. Pharmaceutical companies aren't trying to get you off drugs; they're in business to profit from selling the drugs they manufacture. Pharmaceuticals is a for-profit industry where sick people are the source of profit. Logic and profit margins dictate that healthy people are the last thing they want. Sadly, because most people are unaware of the connections between these government agencies and pharmaceutical companies, they have no idea that the remedy they are being offered is not a cure but a pathway to profit for the agencies and companies involved. They unwittingly believe they are being given healthy solutions, and it's so much easier to take a pill than change their lifestyle.

The great news is that you don't have to sit back and hope for a miracle drug. You can make a better, more difficult decision and commit to doing the things that bring genuine good health.

Drugs are not designed to address the root cause of ailments; they are intended to treat the symptoms of ailments. Any person who has seen or heard an ad for a pharmaceutical drug has listened to the long list of side effects that "could" result from taking just one drug. Most people do not know that the advertised side effects are ACTUAL side effects experienced by a significant number of people in the trial studies of that drug. When you hear a warning of "sudden death," that means people "suddenly died" because of this drug during the trial phase. The FDA, USDA, and pharmaceutical companies know that once you're on a drug, there is a chance it will cause side effects. When you visit the doctor about the symptoms from these side effects, you might be prescribed an additional drug to treat the side effects caused by the first drug. When the second drug causes insomnia, your doctor may prescribe you a third drug, opening the door to a long list of other known and unknown side effects due to the drug itself and the combination of drugs you are now taking. This process continues, effectively making you a lifelong, and sometimes addicted, customer until you die. Advertisements encourage Americans to take drugs, even going to their doctor to request or demand the drugs they take. According to health information research companies, the total number of prescription drugs filled by Americans increased by 85% from 1997 to 2016 while the population only increased by 21%.

The root cause of your original ailment may never be addressed. It may become difficult to remember what your original prescription was treating. I am not telling you to ignore your doctor's advice or to stop taking your medication, but your goal should be to get healthy and stay off drugs. Let's be clear, taking prescription drugs isn't a sin, but it's a weight.

For the record, I am not referring to people born with something like Type I Diabetes. I understand some health interventions are necessary. But if you're reading this and have hip pain and you've opted for painkillers before exercise and stretching, this is for you.

3. FEWER CALORIES IS NOT NECESSARILY THE ANSWER

I don't want your key takeaway to be that you need to get skinny. You can be skinny and unhealthy. Like me, my grandfather was very skinny. He was a hard worker who slaved in a factory his entire life. He was also a heavy smoker who died of lung cancer. He wasn't obese. He was quite well-built, but that didn't prevent him from dying at an early age from smoking.

You can eat fewer calories and have low bone density. Although you look healthy on the outside, you're frail and depleted of necessary vitamins and minerals. You can be skinny and healthy, and you can be skinny and unhealthy.

If you started smoking crack today, you'd be much thinner within a few weeks, but you wouldn't be healthier. Maybe you do need to eat less, but fewer calories won't automatically solve every and all health issues.

4. A HEALTHY LIFESTYLE BRINGS ENERGY, FLEXIBILITY, AND STRENGTH

Have you ever noticed that as people age, they tend to shuffle instead of walk? It's due to a lack of flexibility in their joints. Stretching has the potential to reverse arthritis. Flexibility is the new strength. The more you move, the more energy you'll have. If you ignore flexibility, it will inhibit your ability to move and result in a decrease in energy.

I don't know about you, but I don't want to be tired. I want to have energy. It requires energy to do what God has called you to do. You will be amazed by the increase in your own motivation once you become healthy and have increased energy.

You don't think about growth and increase when you're simply trying to muster up enough energy to get through the day. It takes energy, flexibility, and strength to enjoy life.

5. BE FAIR TO YOUR SPOUSE

Why is it that every time someone gets divorced, they join a gym? Men and women finally start taking care of themselves so they can get remarried. Why didn't you care about your appearance when you were married? Why didn't you value your spouse?

I'm not suggesting that everyone should look like a supermodel. However, it might be a good goal to maintain a human shape for the rest of your life, regardless of your marital status.

It's wrong to let yourself go. Physical attraction should always be present in your marriage. Look good for your spouse.

6. AVOID SODA

The average American diet consists of 60 percent processed foods.[3] It's no surprise the cancer rate continues to climb. As long as Americans continue to eat poorly, the prayer lines will continue to wrap around sanctuaries everywhere.

Don't fall prey to silly marketing schemes. Diet soda is worse than regular soda. Some studies have shown that the ingredients in artificial sweeteners destroy your brain.[4] How do you think all these new diseases manifested all of a sudden? Americans have seen a huge increase in Alzheimer's, Dementia, Diabetes, etc.[5]

The FDA stands for Food and Drug Administration. The USDA stands for US Department of Agriculture. They regulate every aspect of the food you eat that gets you hooked on drugs they regulate, all the while attempting to maintain their benign, if not altruistic, appearance.

There are other substances I will mention later on that I suggest you reduce. I recognize how difficult it is for people to quit anything cold turkey, but soda is something I suggest you get rid of completely. There's no benefit.

I used to keep a 24-pack of Mountain Dew in my refrigerator and just throw them back when I was bored. It was the one thing I made a part of my diet that I felt the Lord speak to me about. He told me I would have problems down the road if I continued to drink them. One day, as I was coming off a fast, I reached for a Mountain Dew, and I could taste the chemicals in it. I attributed my reaction to my recent fast and was planning to power through it until the bad taste went away. Then I thought to myself, 'why am I trying to get back on Mountain Dew?' This might be my one shot to put it down for good. So that's what I did. I highly recommend you do, too.

7. REDUCE OR ELIMINATE FAST FOOD

I understand the appeal of fast food. It's cheap, it's easy, and it's satisfying. But if you eat Chick-fil-A every day, soon enough, you'll need a bigger vehicle.

Fast food doesn't only refer to places with a drive-through. Anything that comes in a box or a bag is fast food. It's highly processed crap. There's no point in living a long life if you're going to struggle through life eating nothing but kale and carrots. That's not what I'm suggesting. Food is to be enjoyed, but most of the "food" found in grocery stores and pedaled through takeout windows wouldn't be recognized as food by your grandmother.

Eat the best you can afford. Junk food may be cheap and satisfying, but it's a waste of money. Eat organic food as much as possible. Consume grass-fed, grass-finished beef, chicken, and eggs, wild-caught fish, and fresh fruits and vegetables. The more quality foods you keep in your refrigerator, the better decisions you'll make. Having the right ingredients in your house makes eating healthier much easier.

8. REDUCE SUGAR

Most people would have a very difficult time eliminating sugar. It's possible to reduce your sugar intake significantly and still indulge occasionally. I'll provide you with an example.

I like iced coffee from Dunkin' Donuts. When you request cream and sugar, the default is four pumps of liquid sugar. I ask for a single pump of sugar when ordering my coffee. If you're well versed in mathematics, you realize I've effectively reduced my sugar intake by 75 percent.

As a rule of thumb, try to eat 5 grams of sugar or less per serving. It has the same effect on your body as having no sugar at all.

9. ELIMINATE ALCOHOL

I think we've entered the twilight zone because unsaved doctors are trying to convince patients to stop drinking alcohol while hipster preachers are promoting alcohol to their congregations. The first thing doctors suggest to patients trying to get healthy is to remove alcohol from their diet.

From a strictly health perspective, it's foolish to think wine has health benefits. All alcohol is toxic. It's a poison. Those who suggest it's acceptable in moderation make a foolish argument.

Ingesting poison in moderation will still kill you, just at a slower rate. Don't reduce alcohol; eliminate it.

Christians don't drink. If you want to live a Christian life and operate in the gifts of the Holy Spirit, abide by what the Bible says about alcohol. Stay away from it.

Both Samson and John the Baptist's parents were told to never allow a strong drink near their sons. Two men who were used for God in a mighty way were required to stay away from alcohol.

10. MOVE

It's not enough to reduce your caloric intake and eat better. You also need to move. God created your body to move. Walking is not enough.

You may notice people out walking every morning, but do you ever notice a difference in their size? It never seems to change much, does it? Decide what type of exercise you can commit to and follow through. It can be a group exercise class like Pilates, cycling, or HIIT (high-intensity interval training). Whatever you choose, stay motivated and adopt it as a part of your lifestyle.

I'm very good at eliminating things that don't benefit me, but it's a challenge for me to add things to my life. If you were to tell me I can't have chicken for the rest of my life, I could do it. But if you told me I have to run 2 miles every morning, that would be very difficult for me. Even when it comes to fasting and prayer, I have a much easier time fasting than I do praying.

I lack the motivation to do things. That's why I hired a personal trainer. I knew if I joined a gym, I wouldn't go. But if I have an appointment with someone who makes their livelihood off of whether I show up, I'll go.

However, you have to trick yourself into being active. It's well worth the effort to cooperate with how God designed your body to function.

11. DON'T BE A DIET FREAK

A select few people in the world have gone the extra mile to achieve optimal health and eliminated sugar from their diet. Some of those who have done this need to reintroduce sugar back into their diet immediately because they're so miserable everyone around them is suffering too.

Don't go on a diet and turn into a jerk. Whatever you introduce or eliminate needs to be sustainable. While you undergo the process of transforming your habits to better your health, go out of your way to treat your family well.

Keep in mind that the same God who instituted fasting also instituted feasting. There are times to enjoy foods that you wouldn't usually eat. You don't have to stand in the corner, angrily eating pistachios at your child's birthday party because you're on a diet. There are times when you should simply enjoy food—Thanksgiving, Christmas, and other special occasions are appropriate times to indulge. I don't suggest eating whatever you want from December 1st to 31st and gaining 71 lbs. But there are days when you should celebrate life guilt-free.

Lastly, don't become obsessed with your diet. You *are* going to die. The goal in walking in divine health isn't to live forever; it's about living a long, fruitful, high-quality life. Control as much as you can, but recognize there will be times when you can't control everything. Even Jesus told His disciples, *"If you enter a town and it welcomes you, eat whatever is set before you"* (Luke 10:8).

12. CONSIDER INTERMITTENT FASTING

Every Christian should be familiar with fasting. If you already participate in fasting at some point throughout the year, you should find intermittent fasting extremely reasonable. I want to challenge you to give intermittent fasting a try for the next 21 days.

It's simple. You eat for 8 hours and drink only water for 16 hours. It sounds easy, but it's a challenge. It is, however, a very doable challenge. You will become hungry during the 16 hours, but the hunger is bearable.

During the 8 hours in which you eat, it's important not to overeat. Eat until you're full. What you eat throughout the 8 hours is also important. Consume lots of fresh fruits and vegetables, grass-fed beef, and healthy fats.

In the 16 hours you don't eat, your body has an opportunity to process food, burn fat, regenerate stem cells, and boost your immune system. Your body is always processing something. When it doesn't have to constantly process food, it begins to rid itself of things that aren't natural.

When you couple intermittent fasting with exercise, you'll see a huge improvement in your health, both in how you look and feel. Fasting has various benefits. Studies have even shown that fasting is more effective than chemotherapy at killing cancer cells.

13. FIGHT SOCIAL NORMS

The moment you decide to implement any of these suggestions, there will be opportunities to abandon what you've committed to do. Fight the temptation to cave to societal pressure to binge eat and focus on the long-term benefits of what you're doing.

People become angry when you won't eat with them. You can go out with people and not eat. I do it all the time. Make up your mind to eat healthy, and don't deviate from that because of pressure.

14. START WHERE YOU ARE, GOD WILL HELP YOU

When I first joined a gym, I was lifting six-pound dumbbells. They weren't even a masculine color. They were lime green rubber weights. I looked goofy. If you were to see me exercise when I first started, you would have thought I was rehabbing from a stroke. That's how weak I was.

That was my beginning point. I've since worked my way up to using 20 lb. dumbbells. The guy next to me uses 75 lb. weights, and that's okay. Everyone has a starting point. Don't focus on how far you need to go. It doesn't matter how overweight you are or how weak your body is right now; just start.

Begin by cutting the things out of your diet that need to go and believe that God will help you. Stop buying crappy food. Stop going to restaurants whose chief marketing tactic is to allow you to eat as much as you want.

If you have a food or alcohol addiction, God can deliver you from it. You can do it. Start today!

I am proud of you in advance for committing to make lasting changes that will impact your health. Not only do you have God's supernatural covenant, but you're also cooperating with His plan to remain in divine health. Congratulations on doing your part.

CONFESSION

Lord, from this day forward, I will do my part to cooperate with You in Your plan for my divine healing. I refuse to let food control me. I will avoid and eliminate things from my diet as Your Spirit leads. I will move my body in a way that will provide me with the energy required to engage in the work You've called me to do. I will obey your voice. I will follow Your instructions with a happy heart. I am not just obedient; I am willing. I thank You for helping me make the changes I need to make, and I thank You for my healing. In Jesus' name, Amen.

QUESTIONS

1. Divine health is a _____ effort between you and God.

2. You can't operate in _____ and expect to live a long, healthy life.

3. What percentage of Americans regularly take prescription medications? _____

4. What is required to do what God has called you to do? _____
_____

5. True or false: Diet soda is better for you than regular soda: _____

6. What types of foods should you eat instead of fast food? _____
_____

7. _____ or less has the same effect on your body as having no sugar at all.

8. Eliminate alcohol. It's a: _____.

9. God created your body to: _____.

10. What has the potential to kill cancer cells faster than chemotherapy? _____
_____

CHAPTER 7

COMMUNION CARRIES POWER

Despite what some may claim, the gospel is not an American gospel—it works everywhere. The gospel didn't even originate in America. Abraham wasn't born in Philadelphia. Isaac wasn't from Harrisburg. Jacob wasn't from Pittsburgh. The gospel originated in the Middle East, and it works in every nation on earth. It worked for Yonggi Cho in South Korea, and it works in Nigeria, home to the largest churches on planet Earth.

The exchange rate in Nigeria is 850 to 1. One US dollar is equal to 850 naira, yet they're able to build and pack out the biggest churches in the world. The Bible works for anyone who's willing to work it, regardless of geographic location.

Never allow anyone or anything to convince you to quit pursuing the promises contained in God's Word. It's not possible for something to be impossible for you. If it's in God's Word, it works.

The Bible says,

> And now, just as you accepted Christ Jesus as your Lord, you must continue to follow him. Let your roots grow down into him, and let your lives be built on him. Then your faith will grow strong in the truth you were taught, and you will overflow with thankfulness. Don't let anyone capture you with empty philosophies and high-sounding nonsense that come from human

thinking and from the spiritual powers of this world, rather than from Christ.

—Colossians 2:6-8

Most ministries in the US and the Western world violate this scripture. The focus of many churches and believers is rooted in human success principles and philosophy. It's rare to hear anyone on Christian television speak about healing without mentioning essential oils or eating organic. I'm not suggesting there's anything wrong with those things, but they have nothing to do with divine healing. Healing is spiritual.

Likewise, communion isn't a natural thing; it's a spiritual matter. It doesn't make any scientific sense to ingest a sip of grape juice and a cracker and expect cancer to dry up in your body. The Bible warns against turning communion into a natural thing. Don't demean communion by reducing it to an event where the Bible is loosely referenced and preceded by a 30-minute self-help seminar. Communion carries spiritual power.

People will sometimes reference Paul's thorn in the flesh when acknowledging their sickness, and it's silly. First of all, the thorn Paul was referring to was not a physical ailment. Secondly, if you think you're receiving Paul's treatment, then show me the Paul-like revelation. Paul's revelation on communion is deep. Spare me the Paul comparisons.

God provided us with physical actions to take to enter into the blessings contained in His Word. Water baptism, communion, and anointing with oil are all receptor points to enter into God's promises.

Communion is not meant to be a time of mourning and sadness. The Passover is an Old Testament type of communion. In the Old Testament, when they ate the meal that night, it ended 430 years of slavery. In addition to being broken out of slavery, all the silver and gold they were denied as slaves were turned over to them, *and* all their sicknesses and diseases were healed. The Bible says there were no sick people among the 1.3 million people in the nation. That means anyone who was sick among them received healing the night they ate the Passover meal.

If you knew you were going to eat a meal and be broken free from every type of bondage in your life and be reimbursed for all your lost wages in silver and gold, would that meal be a sad meal or a happy meal? The only person who was sad during that meal was Satan, and he's the only person who should be sad during communion.

Communion wasn't a happy meal when I was growing up. We were instructed to remember our sins. But the Bible says to forget the past and look forward to those things which are ahead. The communion meal not only brings you into God's power, but it's also a celebration. Although you live on this earth like everyone else, things work differently for you because you've entered into a covenant with God.

When you came to Christ, you were "circumcised," but not by a physical procedure. Christ performed a spiritual circumcision—the cutting away of your sinful nature. For you were buried with Christ when you were baptized. And with him you were raised to new life because you trusted the mighty power of God, who raised Christ from the dead. You were dead because of your sins and because your sinful nature was not yet cut away. Then God made you alive with Christ, for he forgave all our sins. He canceled the record of the charges against us and took it away by nailing it to the cross.

—Colossians 2:11-14

I don't know how anyone can read these verses and say things like, "How many know we're all sinners?" Yes, everyone has sinned—past tense, but that doesn't make you a sinner. In the same way, there's a difference between having drunk alcohol and being a drinker; you have sinned, but if you've received salvation, you're not a sinner. The record of the charges against you was taken out of your possession and nailed to the cross with Christ.

 You live in victory over sin. Sin doesn't live in victory over you.

And having spoiled principalities and powers, he made a shew of them openly, triumphing over them in it.

—Colossians 2:15 (KJV)

Jesus destroyed the power of the Devil. He stripped him of all his power.

You have died with Christ, and he has set you free from the spiritual powers of this world. So why do you keep on following the rules of the world,

—Colossians 2:20

People think they need prayer when they simply need to understand the Bible. You don't battle alcohol; you lack an understanding of what Jesus did for you 2,000 years ago.

What Jesus did laid the foundation for all the freedom you possess. It has nothing to do with how long you pray or fast. You don't have to battle something that doesn't have any power.

Death and life are in the power of the tongue. When you don't know what the Bible says, you end up using your own mouth to give power to things that don't have any power. Don't say, "Alcohol has had a hold on our family for generations, and I'm just next in line." Keep talking like that, and alcohol will always have a hold on you.

Instead, quote the Bible and say, "Thank You, Lord, for stripping the Devil of all his power 2,000 years ago and spoiling principalities and bringing them to shame and embarrassment." You need to realize that this wasn't even a close battle. The Devil was embarrassed by how weak his power is compared to God. That same power that brings embarrassment to the Devil is your power because God lives in you!

> You have died with Christ, and he has set you free from the spiritual powers of this world. So why do you keep on following the rules of the world, such as, "Don't handle! Don't taste! Don't touch!"? Such rules are mere human teachings about things that deteriorate as we use them. These rules may seem wise because they require strong devotion, pious self-denial, and severe bodily discipline. But they provide no help in conquering a person's evil desires.
>
> —Colossians 2:20-23

People attempt to assimilate things into religion because they need to feel a sense of responsibility rather than simply receiving by faith. That's what Lent is. I've yet to speak to a Catholic who can explain Lent. They can't tell me what it does. I've looked it up myself, but no one who participates in Lent can tell me why they do it.

I don't want anyone in the body of Christ to be ignorant of why we take communion or why we do anything we do, for that matter. That's why it was important to me to get this book to you. People find themselves sucked into a form of religion with no faith attached to it. What scripture instructs and explains why you should only eat fish for a day? There isn't one. It's a human philosophy.

Do you know the actual origins of Mardi Gras? If I have to know, so do you. A group of Catholics got together and decided they needed a final outlet for sin before Lent began. So, because they have to go to church the following day, get ashes on their foreheads, and eat fish, they figured, let's all head down to the French Quarter on Tuesday to live like hell, then see a priest on Wednesday. That's religion.

I'm not picking on Catholics. The same religious ideology will cause some Christians to go to the club on Saturday and then attend church on Sunday with their hand stamped, still smelling of smoke and alcohol. They feel bad for what they did the night before, and now, they have to come to church to discipline themselves. That's not the life of faith.

Being present in service is important, but **if the service doesn't provide a direct encounter with the power of God, then you're simply a churchgoer who's going to Hell.** You may come to church addicted and broken, but you're only one service away from discovering that God's Word says He's already shattered every power and principality of darkness. You can live free all the days of your life!

Your freedom doesn't come from being pious or self-deprived. You're free because 2,000 years ago, the rulers of this world thought they were putting the Son of God to death. But they had no idea what they were doing. He shed His blood. It broke the power of sin and set every man and woman free! That's why we take communion.

 Thank You, God, for sending Jesus to spoil the power of the Devil!

A HAPPY MEAL

The blood of Jesus broke every spirit of oppression, sickness, and disease. His precious blood covers everything that pertains to you. It provides you freedom and a way out of every trouble. There is nothing on earth you can face that you don't have the ability to dominate because of the blood of Jesus.

The power and purpose of communion is not well-known throughout the body of Christ. Let's dive into what it truly is and what it does.

The Scriptures say that God is love. The Word of God also says that if you don't exude the God kind of love as a believer, you can't experience God in His fullness. If you're without love, you don't know God because God *is* love.

The word used for love in these scriptures is the Greek word *agape*. The Bible uses four different words for love. *Agape* refers to the Fatherly love of God toward humans as well as humans' reciprocal love for God. This kind of love means *love feast*. It's a table that's prepared. God doesn't just want to love you; He wants you to love Him back.

Communion is a love feast. Everything God was motivated to do for you was because of His desire to have a continual love feast with you. God desires to have a reciprocal relationship with you. God the Father, God the Son, and God the Holy Spirit were in continual commune and fellowship together. Then, they realized they wanted to share their love and decided to create man in their image. They wanted to include you in their love circle. That's what communion is—it's a chance for you to partake in what's occurring in the spirit realm.

God is a symbolic God. He wants you to remember what He did for you. He wants you to remember what it took to bring you into His love feast. He wants you to put Him in remembrance.

In the Old Testament, God would instruct people to erect altars as memorials for what He did in a specific place. In the New Testament, He said, *"Do this in remembrance of me."* Communion is a symbol of your relationship with God. He didn't just give you healing, love, forgiveness, salvation, and redemption. You, too, have to participate in the relationship. You have to do more than simply know it exists. You have to be a receiver of it.

Communion is a way to show God you are in a relationship with Him. You more than know Him. You know and love Him, and you remember what He did for you. When you eat the bread, it becomes the body of Jesus. The grape juice is no longer juice; it's the blood of Jesus. It enters your body and reminds you that you've been saved, healed, delivered, and set free.

God requires your participation. Remember God in your communion. When you remember God, you can never fail. There is nothing you can't overcome when you remember the blood of Jesus. His blood is symbolic of the blood that was shed and the blood that was put on the doorpost when the angel of death passed.

Your remembrance of the blood of Jesus lets every demonic force know, as for me and my house, we will serve the Lord.

If you're battling cancer or any type of sickness or disease in your body and the doctors have told you they don't know how to help your condition, I encourage you to take communion as your prescription. Order the elements on Amazon and take part in remembering what Jesus did for you on the cross.

Communion magnifies God and His work on the cross instead of your pain and issues in your mind or body.

What you magnify matters. When you magnify God and the blood of Jesus, your pain doesn't matter anymore because all you want to do is throw your hands in the air and thank God for delivering you. Thank Him for setting you free and blessing your marriage.

When I went through the most difficult time in my life, and my body was completely shutting down, I took communion 3 to 4 times a day. Yes, you read that correctly. It's not a typo. I did that to remind the Devil that he didn't have me or my body. "No, Satan. This is symbolic of the work that has already been accomplished on the cross, and I walk in the freedom of that today."

Jesus didn't just die on the cross for your sins. He took 39 lashes upon His body so that you would be whole. When you partake of communion, you are healed. You've already been healed. Everything that's broken or malfunctioning in your body falls into proper alignment because the precious blood of God's only Son has set you free. It brought your redemption and made you right with God. The blood that runs through your veins is the blood of Jesus Christ. Anything that doesn't represent life in your body will come back to life when you drink the blood of Jesus Christ. Everything in your blood, central nervous system, and mind is permeated by His precious blood and brought back to life in Jesus' name.

CONFESSION

Heavenly Father, thank You that your Son's blood is upon me and my children. I thank You for healing my body and touching my mind. Jesus, I remember what You did for me on the cross, and I thank You for it. I am taking this opportunity to further my reciprocal relationship with You. I desire a closer relationship with You. I thank You that this month will be a month of unending victory in the mighty name of Jesus Christ!

QUESTIONS

1. What does communion carry?_____

_____

2. Name the only person who should be sad during communion._____

_____

3. Although you live on Earth, things work differently for you. Why? _____

_____

4. Why do we take communion? _____

_____

5. What type of relationship does God desire to have with you? _____

_____

6. Everything God was motivated to do for you was because of:_____

_____

7. Communion provides you the opportunity to do what? _____

_____

8. Communion magnifies _____ instead of

_____.

CHAPTER 8

HEALING TESTIMONIES

CANCER AND KIDNEYS HEALED!

My mother was diagnosed with cancer in her kidneys a little over a week ago. She was in bad shape. It reached the point where she could maybe eat a grape and drink some juice, then throw up.

I appreciate Pastor Jonathan because he cares. I spoke to him after service and told him the real reason I came was because my mother has cancer and I don't want to see her die. He put everything down and he prayed for me. At the end of the prayer he said, "These hands that I'm holding in my hands, if you will leave, go pray, and put these hands on your mother. She will rise and be healed."

I left church happy about what he said. I got to the car and called my wife to let her know I was going to take the two-hour drive to Cabrini Hospital in Alexandria, Louisiana. I arrived at the hospital around 12:30 am on Sunday. I wasn't sure how I was going to get into my mother's room. By that time, visiting hours had been long over. I just happened to notice another door that someone had propped open, and I went right in.

I had already called my brother and told him I was coming. I walked in the door and said, "Mom, I came here with a prayer that the evangelist told me to pray. He told me to put my hands on you and you'll be healed." I laid my hands on her kidneys just like he said. I prayed and I walked out the door believing my mom was healed. I didn't stay for five minutes. I told my mom I'd see her tomorrow, then I left and went to work.

The next morning, my brother called me and said, "Hey, mama's eating!" A couple of days later she ate chicken and cake and drank milk. When the doctors saw that, they ordered 15 tests trying to find the cancer and they couldn't find it!

Bo Johnson, Louisiana

PARALYZED WOMAN HEALED FROM RARE GENETIC DISEASES

I was born with a rare form of muscular dystrophy, as well as mitochondrial disease, which is a genetic defect in every cell of your body. It grows progressively worse with age. About ten years ago, I became dependent on a wheelchair. Using any energy would cause me to become physically sick.

Four years ago, my condition worsened to the point where I was totally bed-bound. I couldn't stand up. When I did, my blood would pool in my feet, a condition called autonomic dysfunction. I required a wheelchair that would hold me up laterally, and I also needed a headpiece to hold my head up. I was placed on daily IV fluids. I required life-sustaining medication for organ function. I was in lots of pain, 24 hours a day with no end in sight. I was also on a ventilator because my diaphragm was so weak that I couldn't take in enough oxygen, which caused the carbon dioxide to poison me. I remember thinking that this was the end.

For four years, I prayed. I didn't know how to get out of this. I loved the Lord. I'm a Bible college graduate. All I could do was pray. I couldn't read my Bible. I couldn't sit up or stand for more than a couple of minutes. I said, "Lord, show me the way to my healing, because I can't believe that you would just pick and choose some people to be healed and not others." It didn't make any sense to me. I asked the Lord to show me the way and to do it in such a way that I can share my testimony so that others might be able to get to that same place of wholeness and healing.

I turned on Daystar, and Pastor Jonathan was on. As I began to listen to him preach, it ignited my spirit and my faith in such a way that I knew I was hearing the message in a different way, in a new way that I hadn't heard before. It wasn't as the world preaches, but as God's Word teaches. Pastor Jonathan taught me that I don't have to wonder if it's God's will for me to be healed, I have been healed.

I started praying a little differently. I began telling myself, 'I have been healed. I am healed. I am whole.' I kept putting God's Word in my heart. I started listening to Jonathan's teaching every day and every night because I could not get enough. I knew that there was truth in what he was teaching.

Suddenly, my body started to line up. I started getting stronger. One day, I noticed I had been standing up in the kitchen for more than three minutes. I was like, "This is new. I don't have to go sit down. This is great."

It was the beginning of August when I came across Jonathan's teachings on Daystar. By the beginning of September, I started to get some strength and was able to function out of my sick bed more often than usual.

I've been a muscular dystrophy patient for many years. I've gone to the same clinic for 16 years and progressively gotten weaker and weaker and sicker and sicker. There is no man-made cure for this disease. It was essentially a death sentence. I had made out my will. I was that horribly sick. On September nineteenth, I went to my muscular dystrophy clinic appointment knowing that I had gained some strength, but I didn't expect what was coming. The occupational therapists came in and checked my shoulders and my hips, which were always weak, and told me they were five plus. I had no idea what that meant. I had never heard of five plus. She told me that five plus is perfect muscle strength!

Next, the respiratory team came in and did their tests. They said, "Your respiratory function is above anything that we can imagine." They recommended my doctor to take me off my ventilator. "Is that okay with you?" they asked. I said, "Yes, absolutely!"

Then they sent my doctor in and she did all of her tests on my legs and all my other functions. She confirmed everything is five plus! There was so much joy on our faces! All I could say was Jesus! It's Jesus. Jesus, Jesus.

Tanya Smith, Florida

39 TUMORS COMPLETELY DISAPPEARED

I attend Choose Life Church in Hobbs, NM. In May, I began having pain in my stomach. Generally, when women have pain in that area, the default response is to do an ultrasound. Women's ovaries are usually about the size of a quarter. The ultrasound revealed I had a cyst the size of a grapefruit inside my ovary, 11 centimeters in diameter. During COVID, all of the oncologists for gynecology had moved out of the area. My doctor at the time felt my condition was serious and referred me to MD Anderson in Houston, Texas – arguably the top Cancer Center in the country.

I met with my church and prayed. I started fasting because I knew in my spirit it was going to be a tough battle for me, but I knew God had already begun to work. November 29th was my first appointment. The scan results showed I had a large eleven-centimeter cyst on my left side and a tumor on my right side. The scan also found tumors on my belly button and on my left side next to the cysts. In just over a month's time, my stomach filled up with fluid, about 40 liters (12 gallons) of water in total. The doctors explained the fluid was caused by irregularities in my lymph nodes. In my lining, there were 39 tumors. I had no idea anything was wrong. I didn't have any pain in that area. I knew a giant was trying to come my way.

When Jonathan came to our winter revival at church, I didn't ask for prayer. Pastor Jonathan saw that my belly was full. He probably thought I was some pregnant girl because I had a perfectly round belly. I didn't look sick. When he prayed for me, I felt something come over me. Pastor Dean and Pastor Jonathan always emphasize that if you get serious with God, God gets serious with you. I decided to go all in with God. That same night, my husband answered the altar call for the first time in our 14-year marriage– he got saved that night. We made the decision that we were going to hit the devil straight in the face and in other private parts.

All throughout November, December, and January we flew and drove back and forth to Houston. I had a second scan in January. The scan took place at a different building with a different machine. This time it showed the tumor started to shrink from eleven centimeters to seven centimeters, but otherwise, my condition was the same. I still had the fluid and 39 other tumors.

I was scheduled to have everything removed to get as much cleaned out before they went in to remove the actual cancer. Before doing so, they did what's called a CA-125 to test my cancer levels. Women my age range between 0 and 34. My count was 658. My doctor told me that if it's cancer, I was most likely looking at stage three, as it seemed to me metastasizing. It was spreading to other parts of my body.

In February, I was back to Houston for a biopsy. It was a Friday night when I received the results of the biopsy–malignant. My heart began to race while having dinner with my family. But in my spirit, God told me no. So, I just gave my husband a look. I showed him the results, held his hand, and I knew this wasn't it.

The next morning at 8 a.m., I received a revision to the test. The results were now classified as "borderline." That meant the tumors were not malignant, they were borderline with the potential to become malignant. God was already showing me he was at work.

At my next doctor's visit, they shared their treatment plan with me. The plan was to remove and clean up as many of the close to 40 tumors in my lymph nodes as possible. Also, to clean up the larger ones on the bottom section of my stomach as well as remove as much of the fluid as possible. I was also told I had colon damage, so they would have to reset my colon and would require a colonoscopy bag for the rest of my life. I was told I would have to do six sessions of chemotherapy. I immediately told her no with a smile on my face. She told me she would give me three weeks to think about it. I just told her no, looked at my husband, and told my husband God would deal with her as I walked away.

While the doctor was telling me the plan, I smiled back at her. Jonathan had already prayed for me. I wasn't in fear. It was to the point that my doctor had to keep asking me if I was understanding what she was saying to me. She scheduled my surgery for February 28th. I agreed and left happy and smiling. The next day, I received a call from the hospital psychologist. They thought I was crazy because I refused to respond to their plans with fear. I rejected the additional assistance the hospital offered for my mind because I knew in whom I had believed.

The night before I was scheduled for surgery, my doctor called me from her personal phone number. Every other call up to this point had been from an MD Anderson recorded line. She told me she knew I wasn't interested in doing chemo, and that she didn't think I required it either. She told me to reject it when I went in for my surgery.

When I went in for surgery, the doctors took out one benign tumor. My doctor described everything else as being "just shadows." There was nothing else there. The 39 tumors were healed by the power of God! I went to MD Anderson three different times to get CT scans to confirm my condition wasn't getting better before they scheduled my surgery. Three different machines. Three different locations. All of them confirmed 39 tumors. I was discharged the same day! When the devil told me to plan for a funeral, I planned for a new home instead!

Marissa, New Mexico

BONUS TESTIMONY FROM MARISSA – ANOTHER CANCER PATIENT HEALED

While my husband and I were in Houston for my CT scan, he met a car dealer whose wife was diagnosed with cancer and was also a patient at MD Anderson. We went to visit him at his car dealership because we were in the market for a new car.

When we arrived, he began to break down and tell us about his wife's battle with cancer. It was in her bone marrow and required a transplant. He mentioned that they had been in and out of church. That's when I completely interjected and stopped their business deal. We joined hands in the middle of the dealership and I told him the same power that was in me would enter into him and onto his wife.

After we prayed, I connected him with Pastor Jonathan's ministry. I helped him download the Revival Today App. I told him Pastor Jonathan had recently visited our church. He asked me what church I went to, and I told him. His jaw hit the floor. As I was walking in, he had to hit pause on his YouTube broadcast. It was Pastor Jonathan preaching at the Choose Life revival in Hobbs!

A few days later, I checked in on him to see if he was watching Pastor Jonathan's broadcasts. He responded with, "My wife is cancer-free!" Praise God!

Marisa, New Mexico

HEART CONDITION HEALED AND LUNGS RESTORED!

I grew up with my sister, Elena. She's five years older than me and she was always in the hospital. She was born with a hole in her heart. When she was five, she had open heart surgery. Then, 25 years later, she had another open-heart surgery.

It's been four years since we got saved, agreed, and prayed for a miracle. We went to many revival meetings and my sister's condition remained the same. One side of her heart functioned at 35% capacity, and the other side, at 37% capacity. In May, blood clots began to develop and my sister suffered a stroke.

The doctors told her another surgery would kill her. Instead, they prescribed medications in an attempt to extend her life. My sister is 51 years old. Doctors gave her no more than ten years to live.

I asked the doctors to provide all of my sister's medical records in English so that she could travel to America to attend this revival meeting. She was able to make the trip with a tremendous amount of medication.

In the meeting, Pastor Jonathan called my sister out of the crowd. Even though he's never met her and knows nothing about her condition, he said two things. "There's something in you that will be healed, but there's something else that requires a miracle, something that needs to be created. Have your sister put her hand on her belly and put the other one on her chest. God is gonna heal you on the inside. And then he's gonna give you a miracle."

Yesterday, my sister received her miracle. This morning, I asked her if there's anything she couldn't do before that she can do now? She told me she was able to climb the stairs without loss of breath. When she told me that, I had her go up and down the stairs again two more times. She was breathing the exact same way I would breathe if I were to climb the stairs twice in a row. Her breathing has returned to normal!

Elena, Switzerland

HEALED FROM LUPUS

Lupus is an autoimmune disease that affects virtually every part of your body. For me, it affected my muscles, joints, heart, and kidneys. I was in so much pain every day. It hurt to brush my teeth and my hair. It hurt to get dressed. I used to have to hold the rail and the steps and basically crawl up the 12 steps in my home to get from my bedroom to the living room.

I went to see Pastor Jonathan preach in New London, Connecticut. He called my husband and me up and prayed for us. He declared I was healed. A week later, I had my blood work done and then went on vacation to Florida for a week. I returned and went to a doctor's appointment and my doctor was confused and astonished. For the first time since my late teens, all my blood work came back normal. She couldn't explain it. She had my bloodwork retested and received the same results.

Now, I can get dressed and walk up the stairs free of pain! It's been three years since I was healed, and I have not been back to the doctor. I get dressed without pain. I fly up and down our stairs, pain free. I thank God every day that I'm healed and that I have no ailments whatsoever!

Jessica, Connecticut

CHRONIC PAIN VANISHED

I have attended Revival Today Church in Pittsburgh since the second week of January. When Pastor Jonathan began 40 Days of Glory, we met every night. One night, I was serving as an usher as Pastor Kofi preached. As I was standing in line for prayer, I received healing, before Pastor Kofi even had a chance to pray for me.

Before that night, my feet hurt so bad I couldn't stand without being in pain. From the moment I stepped out of bed in the morning, walking was a struggle. I was in constant pain. As Pastor Kofi preached, I stood there listening to him pray for someone else. Suddenly, I felt the power of God shoot through my body. It hit my feet and knees and instantly, I knew I was healed.

It's been over a year, and I have not had any pain in my feet since the day I was healed. I can walk normally. I can stand on my feet eight hours a day pain-free. I owe it all to God.

Steve, Pennsylvania

HEART CONDITION HEALED

I had never spoken with Pastor Jonathan before, but he walked up to me and knew there was something wrong with my heart. I've had four heart attacks, nine stints, and two open heart surgeries. I've died twice and been resuscitated. The doctors wanted to operate on me again to put another stint in my heart, but I didn't want to do that. I almost died the last time they attempted it.

My wife began attending Bible study at Foundation Church at a time when I had an 80% blockage in my heart. I accompanied my wife to Bible study one night and the ladies prayed for me. One of them had their son pray for me out in front of the church. This little boy came up to me and punched me in the chest and told the devil to leave and take the blockage with him.

I never had to have the operation. It's all clear. The blockage is gone. When Pastor Jonathan laid hands on me in the middle of a revival meeting, I felt something flow through me. It felt hot. Immediately, I could tell the difference in my heart. It's completely healed and restored. I don't have any more cramping in my back where I used to have the heart attacks. My wife is a nurse. She took my blood pressure and it's way lower than it's been.

John, Florida

BLIND EYE RESTORED

I had a problem with my eye. I've had four surgeries in an attempt to heal a detached retina. I was recommended to a new doctor because mine gave up and said there was nothing more he could do. The new doctor performed a fifth surgery and when all was said and done, I still couldn't see out of it.

Up until last night, all I could see out of my right eye was complete darkness. I could feel the scar tissue in my eye every time I blinked my eye. Last night at the revival meeting, my eyesight was restored. I realized during the meeting that I could see all the holes in my wife's shirt (they were intentionally there). When I cover what used to be my "good eye" I can still see!

I didn't mean to doubt God. I don't doubt Him. I've learned not to. While Pastor Jonathan was still preaching, I closed my good eye and started walking through the rows, just because I could!

Cody, Florida

WOMAN HEALED OF LEUKEMIA

I was diagnosed with leukemia 13 years ago. I've been battling the disease, taking medication to keep my blood levels under control, but the medication's side effects made me very weary. My doctor suggested that I pause taking the medication that was causing side effects to see what would happen. Shortly after Pastor Jonathan laid hands on me and prayed, I went for a PET Scan. The results of that scan were clear! I no longer have leukemia, I'm healed! I'm so blessed and completely blown away. I want to share my story with anyone who needs to hear it. If God did it for me, I know He will do it for anyone.

Joyce, Pennsylvania

YOUNG MAN RESTORED AFTER SEVERE ACCIDENT

My youngest brother has suffered from epilepsy for 10 years. Dehydration caused him to fall and hit his head during a race when he was in the 8th grade. His central nervous system has gradually declined ever since. He could not recollect memory, understand speech, or maintain his balance. He couldn't control his movements in any way, shape, or form. Perhaps the worst part of all was that he could not sleep. Every ten minutes or so he would have a seizure, or twitch. He could not enjoy the REM state of sleep because he would experience a major attack every few hours. It was an oppression of the devil. My parents hadn't had a good night's sleep in ten years. They had to alternate every hour to ensure my brother's safety. We attempted to teach my brother the Word of God and pray with him, but he just wasn't there. My brother, the presidential honor roll student was reduced to a second-grade memory.

When we heard that Pastor Jonathan was going to be in Los Angeles, it was an answer to prayer. We began to believe that my brother's oppression would end in that meeting. We arrived expecting and believing the Lord for a miracle. We came prepared and full of faith. We had just completed 21 days of prayer and fasting with Revival Today Church, we prepared a special offering to the Lord as proof of our expectation of the miracle He was going to perform.

During the meeting, Pastor Jonathan called spoke to every member of my family, and the word of knowledge he delivered for my brother was spot on. It was so accurate. He said that the Lord was going to restore his speech, his movement, and everything the enemy had stolen from him. Pastor Jonathan then asked my brother if he wanted prayer, he responded and said yes! Then, he stood without assistance! Both acts were things my brother was unable to do. The Lord touched him.

My family and I were amazed. We went home rejoicing and praising God. That night he was able to sleep longer than he's ever been able to since the accident! You could see the spirit of peace upon his life. We're so excited to see what God has done and how He will continue to restore my brother completely, from the top of his head to the soles of his feet. His bodily function, memory, intellect, everything is coming back to him, and we give God all the praise, glory, and honor.

Mikey, California

TODDLER HEALED FROM RESPIRATORY ATTACK

My four-year-old son was diagnosed with eczema when he was very young. The disease caused him to have respiratory episodes, making it difficult for him to breathe. The incidents would drain him of his strength and energy as he fought to breathe. When he was younger and experienced an episode, we would rush him to the hospital, where they would give him medication, steroids, and place him on a respirator until his breathing normalized.

I attend Bible School at RBTI. I was reading *Christ the Healer* by TL Osborne for one of my classes when my son had another episode. My wife told me to get my son's respirator like usual, but this time I told her no. I began to pray for him instead. I took oil from my kitchen, lifted my son's shirt, and used it to lay hands on my son. I commanded the inflammation to stop and for his breathing to align with God's Word. When I didn't see immediate results, I remembered what I read in *Christ the Healer*. Our senses, the things we see and hear, fight against our faith. It's imperative to remain in faith despite our senses. As I paced the room, I realized my son's shirt was pulled up, exposing his irregular breathing as I prayed.

The day before the incident occurred, Pastor Augustine gifted me a suit, originally given to him by Pastor Jonathan. I heard the Holy Spirit tell me to get the jacket and lay it over my son. I did it and continued praying. I prayed all night until I eventually fell asleep. The next morning when I woke up, my son's breathing had returned to normal. It was the first time he'd ever recovered from an episode without medication and a respirator! I am so thankful for Revival Today Ministries and Pastor Jonathan. I give God all the glory, honor, and praise.

AJ, Pennsylvania

ANSWER KEY

CHAPTER 1

1. They have not received the Word of God to illuminate the darkness in their lives.

2. The confidence you can have in Him comes from His Word.

3. God's will found in His Word.

4. He's done everything He can do. He sent His Son to die on the cross to bring healing.

5. Will

6. To walk in divine health/ walk whole and healed all the days of your life.

7. You receive healing as a free gift from God, now.

8. Believe in your heart + Confess with your mouth + Receive = God's Promise.

CHAPTER 2

1. Spiritual

2. The spiritual realm is more real than what you see in the natural realm because our natural realm can only produce what is done in the spirit realm.

3. You have to first receive it spiritually.

4. Satan is your enemy. His purpose is to kill, steal, and destroy.

5. Jesus views sickness as oppression from the Devil. Acts 10:38 says, *"Then Jesus went around doing good and healing all who were oppressed by the Devil, for God was with Him."*

6. Double restoration

7. a) delivered b) disgusted

8. a) sickness b) sin

CHAPTER 3

1. God has already given me everything pertaining to life and godliness (2 Peter 1:3).

2. Paul's prayer was that the church would understand what already belongs to them.

3. a) spirit b) soul c) body

4. When you receive faith for healing in your spirit, it will manifest in your body.

5. Matthew 21:21

6. You have the faith to believe for your healing because you were given the faith for it by God.

7. 1) unbelief 2) faith

8. a) amplify b) override

9. *"then I will not make you suffer any of the diseases I sent on the Egyptians; for I am the Lord who heals you." Exodus 15:26; "I will bless you with food and water, and I will protect you from illness." Exodus 23:25; "He also brought them out with silver and gold, and there was none feeble among His tribes." Psalms 105:37.*

10. Unbelief.

11. You come to the realization that you cannot do it on your own and with your strength and power. You release it and no longer allow it to have any effect on your mind.

CHAPTER 4

1. The knowledge and understanding found in God's Word.

2. Because people are ignorant of what God's Word says belongs to them.

3. Implement the wisdom God has given you in His Word in your everyday life so you'll know exactly what to do.

4. Wisdom is the correct use of knowledge.

5. It causes you to walk in power and dominion.

6. It must bow to the name of Jesus.

CHAPTER 5

1. Have hands laid on you in prayer.

2. Obey God's Word.

3. Keep yourself from speaking evil.

4. The grace of God on your life.

5. A manifestation of God's power on your life.

6. Anger.

7. Destroy your life in a moment of weakness.

8. Rested.

9. Joy.

10. Start with gratitude.

11. The regard you have for your life.

CHAPTER 6

1. Cooperative

2. Gluttony

3. 70 percent

4. Energy

5. False. The sweetener in diet soda destroys your brain and is linked to diseases such as Alzheimer's, Dementia, and Diabetes.

6. Consume grass-fed beef, wild-caught fish, and fresh fruits and vegetables.

7. 5 grams of sugar

8. Poison

9. Move

10. Studies have even shown that fasting is more effective than chemotherapy at killing cancer cells.

CHAPTER 7

1. Spiritual power

2. Satan

3. Because you've entered into a covenant with God.

4. 2,000 years ago, the rulers of this world thought they were putting the Son of God to death. But by the shedding of His blood, the power of sin was broken, and every man and woman was set free!

5. A reciprocal relationship.

6. His desire to have a continual love feast with you.

7. Partake in what's occurring in the spirit realm.

8. a) God and His work on the cross b) your pain and issues in your mind or body.

NOTES

CHAPTER 3

1. 1 Dake, F. J. (2014). Dake's Annotated Reference Bible-KJV. Dake Publishing.

CHAPTER 6

1. https://www.theguardian.com/us-news/2019/may/28/bread-additives-chemicals-us-toxic-america

2. https://newsnetwork.mayoclinic.org/discussion/nearly-7-in-10-americanstake-prescription-drugs-mayo-clinic-olmsted-medical-center-find/

3. https://www.cdc.gov/pcd/issues/2018/17_0265.htm

4. https://bebrainfit.com/neurotoxins-foods/

5. https://www.alz.org/media/Documents/alzheimers-facts-and-figures.pdf; https://pubmed.ncbi.nlm.nih.gov/33756057/; https://www.prb.org/resources/fact-sheet-u-s-dementia-trends/; https://www.cdc.gov/media/releases/2022/p1229-future-diabetes-surge.html; https://www.cdc.gov/diabetes/data/statistics-report/index.html; https://www.cdc.gov/diabetes/health-equity/diabetes-by-the-numbers.html

"My generation shall be saved!"

—Jonathan Shuttlesworth

ABOUT THE AUTHORS

Evangelists Jonathan and Adalis Shuttlesworth are the founders of Revival Today, a ministry dedicated to sharing the Gospel of Jesus Christ with lost and hurting people worldwide.

As Pastor, Jonathan Shuttlesworth launched Revival Today Church in 2022 as a soul-winning, Holy Spirit-honoring church that is unapologetic about believing the Bible is intended to bless families and nations.

Each day thousands of lives are impacted globally through Revival Today Broadcasting and Revival Today Church, located in Pittsburgh, Pennsylvania.

While methods may change, Revival Today's heartbeat remains for the lost, providing biblical teaching on faith, healing, prosperity, freedom from sin, and living a victorious life.

If you need help or would like to partner with Revival Today to see this generation and nation transformed through The Gospel, follow these links…

CONTACT REVIVAL TODAY

www.RevivalToday.com
www.RevivalTodayChurch.com

Get access to our 24/7 network, Revival Today Global Broadcast. Download the Revival Today app from the Apple App Store or Google Play Store. Watch live on Apple TV, Roku, Amazon Fire TV, and Android TV.

Call: 412-787-2578

facebook.com/revivaltoday
x.com/jdshuttlesworth
instagram.com/jdshuttlesworth
youtube.com/@jonathanshuttlesworth

DO SOMETHING TODAY THAT WILL CHANGE YOUR LIFE FOREVER

Thus saith the Lord, **MAKE THIS VALLEY FULL OF DITCHES**. For thus saith the Lord, Ye shall not see wind, neither shall ye see rain; Yet that valley shall be filled with water... **THIS IS BUT A LIGHT THING IN THE SIGHT OF THE LORD**... And it came to pass... **THE COUNTRY WAS FILLED WITH WATER**.

2 Kings 3:16-18; 20

Revival is the only answer to the problems of this country - nothing more, nothing less, nothing else.

Thank you for standing with me as a partner with Revival Today. We must see this nation shaken by the power of God.

You cannot ask God to bless you first, prior to giving. God asks you to step out first in your giving - and then He makes it rain. We are believing God for 1,000 people to partner with us monthly at $84. Something everyone can do, but a significant seed that will connect you to the rainmaker.

IF YOU HAVE NOT YET PARTNERED WITH REVIVAL TODAY, JOIN US TODAY!

This year is not your year to dig small ditches. When I grew tired of small meetings and altar calls, I moved forward in faith and God responded. God is the rainmaker, but you must give Him something to fill. It's time for you to move forward! **Will you stand with me today to see the nations of the world shaken by the power of God?**

Revivaltoday.com/give

revivaltoday.com/paypal

Zelle info@revivaltoday.com

 @RTgive

Text "RT" to 50155
Call at (412) 787-2578

Mail a check to:
Revival Today P.O. BOX 7
PROSPERITY PA 15329

REVIVAL TODAY
Email: info@revivaltoday.com

www.ingramcontent.com/pod-product-compliance
Lightning Source LLC
Chambersburg PA
CBHW060939170426
43194CB00027B/2996